# DR. MATT'S
# **Gutsy Guide**
# to Reading
# in College

## UNLOCKING THE ART OF
## ADVANCED READING

## Dr. Matt Friesen, PhD

For permission requests, contact:
Dr. Matt's College Guides
P.O. Box 492
Independence, OR 97351
www.gutsycollege.com

For Ordering Information:
Special discounts are available on quantity purchases by educational institutions, associations, and others. For details, contact the publisher at the address above.

ISBN: 979-8-9890562-0-0 (Softcover)
LCCN: 2023918342

Book design by Shelby Gates
Printed in the United States of America.

# Acknowledgements

Profound thanks to the hundreds of students, faculty and staff at the University of Oregon, Bluffton University, and Western Oregon University. Your insights, questions, and suggestions made this project possible. Thank you to the Office of Equity and Multicultural Services team at the Oregon Department of Human Services, whose commitment to equity inspires a daily dose of authenticity and hope.

Thank you to wise editorial and creative design work provided by Adria Carey Peres, Rachel Randall, and Shelby Gates.

Finally, and most importantly, thanks to my partner and children, whose encouragement and patience with many hours of noise-canceling headphones and trips to the coffee shop created space and courage to read, write, and bring this book to life.

# Table of Contents

*Dr. Matt's Gutsy Guide*
*to Reading in College*

# Introduction

Right before our university's winter break, three of my Introduction to Sociology students came to my office in tears.

1. Lilly was the first in her family to go to college. She was working hard. Finishing her degree would be great for her, inspire her younger brothers, and support her family in the years ahead. But no one had ever explained how the college routine worked, and the reading and study load was more than she had expected. She was struggling to keep up.

2. José was working full-time and sticking his toe back into college after being out of school for ten years. He, too, was a committed student but faced some serious headwinds. He was sure that going back to school was a great way to take care of his family, but between getting his kids to swim practice and helping them with their homework, he had little time for his own course reading. And on top of that, he didn't know how to ask his family for the support he needed.

3. Tanika was straight out of high school, where she had been a fantastic student who went above and beyond when it came to her studies, sports, and other activities.

But this reading load was really kicking her butt. She was used to reading everything and acing every test, but that strategy wasn't working anymore. Both her grades and spirits had taken a big hit last semester.

Going to college takes guts. Lilly, José, and Tanika were all strong students and committed to doing well in college. But they were also overwhelmed with the work, especially the reading. They were sinking, felt like everyone else knew something they didn't, and were considering dropping out. It wasn't because they couldn't do the work but because no one had taken the time to walk them through how to be great readers in college. If you're feeling a bit like Lilly, José, or Tanika, it's time to change that.

Most students I've encountered over the years can read well, but they never learned how to read *in college*. Reading in college and deciphering the material is essential for graduating and succeeding in a career. No one explained how different readings are set up or why professors choose the readings they do. Nobody walked them through how to take notes on readings or how to organize their space and people to maximize their time. This book covers all these essentials in one place.

Why am I writing this? Because I've been there. On my way to completing my PhD and becoming a university professor, I was a college student facing the same questions. I remember being straight out of high school and adjusting to the college reading load. Later in life, when I returned to school, I learned how to reorganize my plans for studying, working, getting the kids to swim practice, making dinner, and attending parent-teacher conferences.

Over the past decade, I've designed reading lists for dozens of classes. I've talked with hundreds of beginning and advanced students about college reading strategies. I've taught thousands of students in the classroom. And of course, I've spent tens of thousands of hours on my own reading. Along the way I've spent a lot of time thinking about the best ways to read different genres, and I have worked with students to fine-tune their note-taking and organizing strategies. In short, I'm sort of a reading geek.

And here's the thing about why learning to read well is so important: reading is the foundation of college success and life afterwards. Every class you take in college will include reading. Some will have more; some will have less. It will all be slightly different, but every test, project, paper, and assignment in college will require reading. (BTW, I know that right now you may be trying to think of classes that won't have any reading. But trust me, even the volleyball and tai chi classes I took in college had some reading.)

After graduation, when you've started your career, every blueprint, employee evaluation, and instruction manual will require you to read carefully. The further you go in your career, the more important it will be to read not just for information, but as a creative and critical thinker. I've written this book to help you get great grades in school and prepare you for the life that follows.

In fact, I'll give you a reading hint right now that will pay for the cost of this book. Without exception, the main reason students in my classes lost points on papers they wrote was because they did not carefully read the assignment. Yes, some lost points for hideous grammar or because they forgot to run a spell check. Some plagiarized or turned in their assignment late. But most students lost points because *they did not take a few minutes to carefully read the assignment*. If you learn nothing more from this book than to take some time to read your assignments more carefully, you will have increased your grade point average by at least half a point.

## What You'll Find Here

Fair warning. This book is not about speed-reading or power-cramming. This book is about learning how to figure out what to focus on in the reading. This book will teach you how to improve your recall for exams. It will explore new ways to take notes and organize your life and reading. If you work these ideas into your routine and reading strategies, you will not only see your grades improve but also discover some entirely new ways to make reading part of your life.

How are we going to do this? If you just want reading tips and tricks, I'm happy to save you some time (and a few dollars). You can find page after page of clever ideas on the internet about how to read. But if you really want to change your reading in a way that will change the way you study, you'll find it here.

In Chapter 1, we'll take a short walk through what we know about reading. What happens in your brain when you read? How do you read in ways that will help you remember? How are kids' and adults' brains different, and what does this mean for how you learn and read?

Chapter 2 digs deeper into what reading looks like *in college* and how it's set up in specific ways. We'll look at what professors are thinking when they assign readings, how difficult college reading really is, and how to recognize different types of reading. Understanding what's going on behind the college reading curtain will help you know how reading fits into your whole academic adventure.

Chapter 3 is about setting yourself up to be an excellent college reader. This is an essential step that most students never think about. Here you'll learn how to set up your state of mind, schedule, space, people, and technology. These steps alone will dramatically improve your college reading and probably your grades.

Chapter 4 gets to the heart of our reading work. In addition to those perennial questions about the usefulness of highlighters, flash cards, and the pros and cons of reading off paper versus screens, we'll unpack a dozen different note-taking strategies and the particular ways to use these as you work through textbooks, academic articles, novels, and other types of reading.

Chapter 5 wraps up with some thoughts on reading that you've probably never heard. These perspectives take you well beyond the reading strategies in the first four chapters and will not only impress your professors with your insightful questions, but will also change the way you look at everything you read. If you take them seriously, they might just change your life.

# How to Use This Book

This book is designed to give you both excellent information about reading in college and practical tools that you can start using right now.

Here are three steps for how to get the most out of this book:

1. First, read the whole thing from cover to cover. It's shorter than much of what you'll encounter in your classes, and you'll find tools and perspectives to strengthen your reading from the beginning to end.

2. Next, work through the "setting up" chapters in Chapter 3. Don't get too perfectionistic about it. Also, remember that the accompanying free downloadable workbook found at gutsycollege.com will give you tools to work through the setting up. Think about the areas where you have your life put together, and then do a bit of work in places where you need some help. For instance, maybe you've got your study space and tech all figured out, but you haven't sat down with your family to talk about what your return to school will mean for everyone's weekly routines.

3.  Finally, once you have a feel for the book's content and have yourself set up, try this system as you encounter your next college reading:

    - If you haven't already, go to page 47 in Chapter 2 and review "Why Should I Care About the Syllabus?" Then, read the syllabus. Then, when you're finished, read the syllabus again. You get the idea.

    - Go to page 59 in Chapter 2 and review the "What Will I Be Reading in College?" section. Ask yourself what type of reading it looks like you'll be working on.

    - Go to page 118 in Chapter 3 and review the different ideas for taking notes and which ones work best for different types of readings. Choose the strategies that work best for you, and get started. Don't forget to hop over to gutsycollege.com and download the reading template. It is a preformatted .docx document that you can save and adapt, and you will see examples of all the note-taking styles described here.

    - Go to page 139 in Chapter 3 and, if you haven't already, decide how you are going to file your notes. You are putting high-quality time and money into your education and future. It would be a shame to waste it because you misplaced your hard work!

Once you've moved through this process a few times, it will not only become easier, but you'll begin to see how this organization saves you time and improves your grades. For instance, just think how much your papers will improve with the high-quality reading notes you'll be accumulating! This book is designed to not just be read through and put on your shelf, but used as a guide to help you design your own best reading discipline.

Whether you are 18 or 58, are getting ready to head to school or are already there, this book is for those of us who have struggled with reading and keeping the rest of our lives in balance. If you work these strategies into your routine and stick with them, you'll see your grades improve, impress your professors, pick up some great career-building habits, and might just learn a few new things about yourself.

In addition to the in-depth information you'll find here, make sure to visit the accompanying website, gutsycollege.com. The site provides more learning hints and free downloadable reading tools and templates that accompany these chapters. You can customize these resources to make your reading and studying even more efficient. Read on!

# CHAPTER 1

# *What We Know About Reading*

**B**efore jumping right into the hints and habits that will make you a college reading machine, it's worth learning some foundational things about reading. What most people don't know is that a lot of research has gone into reading and learning. Knowing a little about how this works can make a huge difference in your college reading success.

I've been through college and graduate school, taught college and university classes, and worked with students to apply their coursework to career planning. These are the things I wish someone would have told me years ago! In the following four sections, we're going to look at a reading blueprint, some reading mindsets, what adults bring to their reading, and how to leverage brain science to make our reading effective. Together, these discoveries will lay a foundation for the next section, which explores what we know about reading *in college*.

# Bloom's Blueprints

Although you may not have handled blueprints, you've probably seen them in movies. Blueprints are the big rolled-out diagrams of buildings that bank robbers and secret agents use to plan how they're going to break into a casino or super-secret vault to install a computer virus that will transfer zillions of dollars into their bank accounts or end the world. Blueprints give you a bird's-eye view of how something was put together so you can see where you want to go.

Action/thrillers aside, the real purpose of blueprints is to help construction workers understand how to build a building. Blueprints detail what materials to use and what tools are needed to fit the hardware together. Blueprints diagram the order of construction so no one begins working on the roof before the basement is finished. There are lots of rules and building codes that dictate how things are to be built, but every set of blueprints and construction project is still unique.

Wouldn't it be great if we had blueprints for reading in college? If we had a way to understand how reading expectations were put together so we knew what to look for and could take the right tools with us to find our way through the hallways, air vents, and secret doors of our classes?

Looking at the reading blueprints is an essential but typically overlooked step in college reading success. Understanding why you're reading something and what the professor wants you to get out of it can save you hours of time and help you focus on what you most need to master for papers and exams.

## Discovering Bloom's Blueprints

One of the foundational guides to reading and learning is Bloom's Taxonomy[1]. (Quick sidenote: looking up words you don't know is an excellent reading habit. In the meantime, if you didn't know it before, now you do: "taxonomy" means the science of classifying stuff.)

I'm sure you will be shocked to learn that it is named after Benjamin Bloom, and it was developed as a way to think about how learning can be organized and moves from more foundational to more advanced ways of reading and learning.

When I became a college professor, the ideas behind Bloom's Taxonomy changed the way I thought about how I mapped out my classes and student reading expectations. This image shows how it works[2].

# Bloom's Taxonomy

**create** — Produce new or original work
Design, assemble, construct, conjecture, develop, formulate, author, investigate

**evaluate** — Justify a stand or decision
appraise, argue, defend, judge, select, support, value, critique, weigh

**analyze** — Draw connections among ideas
differentiate, organize, relate, compare, contrast, distinguish, examine, experiment, question, test

**apply** — Use information in new situations
execute, implement, solve, use, demonstrate, interpret, operate, schedule, sketch

**understand** — Explain ideas or concepts
classify, describe, discuss, explain, identify, locate, recognize, report, select, translate

**remember** — Recall facts and basic concepts
define, duplicate, list, memorize, repeat, state

The idea here is that our college reading blueprints reveal multiple floors. As we move through our courses, we are building one floor on top of the next. Your early classes will typically start at the first floor and become more complex as you work up to the second, third, and higher stories.

The foundational floors will likely emphasize learning basic facts and concepts. The reading will have more of an overview feel to it, will feel like a manageable number of pages, and probably won't be too difficult. At this stage, flash cards and other tools for memorizing material can be especially useful.

The middle floors will ask you to build on these early foundations, challenge you to apply what you've read to new situations, and ask you to compare readings to each other to see how they are similar or different. A favorite assignment of professors in these middle floors is to ask you to compare and contrast two or more readings. This means looking for several common themes in the readings and explaining how they are similar and different.

Finally, as you begin to put the finishing touches on your academic construction project, you will learn how to apply all this learning to new situations and begin crafting your own new body of work or explore ideas that spur innovation. Many programs (including the one I taught in) required a senior or capstone project where students took something they were particularly interested in and applied what they had learned throughout all the floors of their work. The readings associated with these projects were specific to the student. This is where students can begin to surpass their professors' knowledge in these areas.

I don't want to paint a picture here that is sharply divided. Although it's obvious when you move from the eighth to the ninth floor in a hotel, these academic stories often blend into each other in college. Introductory classes will likely ask you about compare-and-contrast concepts. Advanced courses will still be challenging you with new vocabulary. But in general, you will see this pattern of foundational material leading to more advanced readings as you move through your courses.

## *Implications of Bloom's Blueprint*

In addition to showing us that reading comes in many forms and with many different purposes, Bloom's blueprint shows us even more:

- **We need to get things in the right order.**
  Before we jump into a challenging reading, we need to have the basics well in hand. We need to invest in memorizing facts and looking up the definitions of words we don't know. BTW ... there is no shame in this! If you don't know what a word means, look it up. I remember how relieved I was when one of my advisors told me that when she went back to graduate school for her PhD in Sociology, she kept her dictionary app open on her phone when she read because she was constantly using it. Remember, looking up words doesn't mean you're ill-prepared; it means you're doing the work. It's when

you're not looking up words that you're falling down on the job.

- **Bloom gives you a look inside the professor's head.**
  Whether or not your professor has specifically used Bloom's Taxonomy to design the class, they are doing it intuitively, starting with overviews and moving into details, beginning with simpler concepts and building to more complex ones. For instance, in my sociology program we began with *Introduction to Sociology*, then moved to *Social Theory* and *Social Science Methods*, then more specific subfields such as *Social-psychology* and *Gender Studies*, and finally on to students' specific areas of interest and their graduation projects. Each step builds on the previous one.

- **Reading difficulty follows a similar pattern.**
  You'll typically find that as you move from the first and second to the fourth and fifth floors of your courses, the reading difficulty will increase. Professors now trust that you understand the basic concepts and can handle more complicated ideas. This is also why some courses have "prerequisites." The professor has decided that you need to understand and pass a more foundational class before you take a more advanced one.

## *Beyond Bloom's Blueprints*

Bloom's blueprints are fantastic. They give you a good sense of what to expect as you move through your classes. But they are still a bit general. How do you get a clearer idea of where your reading is headed in your classes?

Here are four ideas that will add more detail to your personal reading blueprints:

1. Do your own homework. In addition to your class assignments, set aside a few minutes to explore the field more broadly. Although I don't recommend it as a research source, try doing some Wikipedia searches. These entries often give broad overviews in just a few pages. I think of Wikipedia as an extended dictionary entry. You'll likely get a good sense of the broad themes of your class.

2. Read the syllabus. Of course you've done that already ... right? Often, professors will give an overview of the reading expectations in the class syllabus. Unfortunately, many students don't take the time to read this critical resource. More on this later!

3. Visit the professor and teaching assistants (TAs). Visiting during your professor's or TAs' office hours is another underutilized resource. Most of the time, they use their office hours for grading because nobody comes by. I'd not recommend going by every week, but two to three times throughout the semester is not too much. Bring the questions that will clarify your blueprint.

4. Adjust your reading and note-taking strategy. Now that you understand Bloom's blueprint, you can see

it's essential that you change the way you read and take notes as you build your upper floors. Where early on it was crucial to get facts and learn foundational perspectives, as you build on these classes you need to shift to applying and analyzing concepts. For instance, I remember a very frustrated student coming to my office. She was acing her early sociology classes because she had mastered the use of flash cards. But this wasn't enough in more advanced classes. Together we explored new ways of reading and taking notes that could help her make connections among ideas rather than just memorizing them.

It can be easy to begin a university class by just showing up at the worksite, putting on your hard hat, grabbing a hammer, and starting to nail things together. But before you find yourself with something that looks like a tornado-thrashed janky doghouse, take a few minutes to look at the blueprints. How does this class fit into your plans? What questions do you want to take to your professor? What sort of reading are you going to encounter, and what is the best way to move through it?

Pausing at the beginning of the class to think about how this building project is going to work will save you hours of study time and probably improve your grades. This small investment will prevent you from working for months on your personal construction site only to find yourself at the bottom of a hole you've dug with no way to get out.

# Managing Our Mindset

When I was in college, I remember complaining about my classes. It just seemed like the thing to do. I criticized one for being too boring, another for being too hard, and another for being disorganized. In hindsight, it was probably less about the class or the professor as it was about me trying to bond with classmates through our common hardship.

Having done the student and professor thing for most of my life, I confess that I've probably taught some boring, difficult, or disorganized classes, too. Professors can get lazy, run out of clever ideas, or find themselves overwhelmed with administrative or other university responsibilities. Not trying to make excuses here, just saying.

I've also learned that while engaging professors and enthralling classes can be much easier to learn in, students also have a lot of control over how much they get out of a class. The perspective we bring to learning is crucial and is as important as the professor's charisma or the readings' quality.

According to Dr. Ken Bain, author of *What the Best College Students Do*, students bring one of three mindsets to their learning (and in our case, reading).[3] Using Bain's three learning mindsets, we can sketch out what these might mean for our reading. We'll also consider a few realities that college students of all sorts face when trying to decide how we approach our reading.

But first, let's look at the mindsets.

## Three Mindsets

When Bain talks about "mindsets," he means the intentions we bring to what we're learning or reading. What are we hoping to get out of this? How much of an effort are we going to make, and how engaged are we going to be? Beyond just skimming through these next couple of ideas, this is a good place to pause and be honest with yourself. What are you really doing in college? What are you really hoping to get out of your studies?

- **Surface Reading**
  Bain suggests there are three ways to approach our studies. The first he calls "surface reading." This is where students do just enough to get by, or as Bain describes it, "Doing just enough to avoid the F." Surface reading is doing the bare minimum: half-heartedly reading the headings, quickly skimming a chapter in the textbook, or looking for a quick summary that lets you get away with as little as possible. When exams come around, it's about cramming, getting just enough to pass tomorrow's pop quiz. Little if anything you read "sticks," and it certainly doesn't connect with something deeper or help you lay a learning foundation you'll build on later.

- **Strategic Reading**
  The second mindset is "strategic reading." Think of it as a step up from surface reading. Bain describes it as "doing just enough to get the A." Sounds good, right? After all,

that's what taking classes is all about. Getting good grades! Yeah … no. Strategic readers may be getting more out of their reading than surface readers, but it's still not striking a deeper chord. Reading is still primarily in response to outside pressures to get grades. Good grades, but it's still about the grades.

- **Deep Reading**
  Bain's third category, "deep reading," launches us beyond grades and draws us into real thinking and growth. Deep reading is driven by our questions, not class grades. Deep reading is about curiosity, not about surviving the midterm. It's about bringing our questions and looking for new ways of thinking about things. Since this mindset is a little harder to explain, let's try a story.

When I was in college, I was interested in why people do what they do, so I took a social-psychology class. One of our readings had to do with how people's decisions are influenced by others around them. I used to think that, sure, people around me probably influenced me a little bit, but not very much. I mean, at the end of the day, I still make my own decisions, right? But I started reading all these studies about how incredibly powerful our social circles are.

I remember reading one study that showed how the worst place to have a heart attack and need help is where there are lots of people. Huh? I figured if I was having an emergency, the more people around the better, right? But it turns out that research has shown that if there are lots of people around and someone needs help, most people will resist stepping forward to avoid the spotlight or they assume someone else will take care of it. This "bystander effect" means that the best place to have a heart attack is where there are only a few people around ... because they are much more likely to rush to your aid. All of this is to say that this was deep reading for me. I was intrigued, amazed, and still remember this bit of information many years later.

Deep reading happens when you find a way to connect with a reading beyond surviving the midterm exam or cobbling together enough points to get an A in the class. Deep reading helps you carry foundational information up to the next story of your academic architecture (thank you, Bloom!) and later into your career.

## A Deep-Reading Strategy

One section of Bain's book specifically addresses how we should read in college. I've summarized his list of eleven strategies for deep reading as a set of questions.

As you read, ask yourself:

1. What is this reading about, and how it will challenge me?

2. What do I expect to find in this reading? After I've finished, was it what I thought? Why or why not?

3. After a quick scan, what are the purpose, structure, and main points of the reading? What questions is it trying to answer?

4. How does this reading connect with other things I'm reading and learning?

5. With fiction, ask: What are the big questions this reading is working with? How does this work touch me?

6. With nonfiction, ask: What are the arguments, and do the conclusions flow from them?

7. What is the evidence? Are there other ways to understand this evidence?

8. Where does this reading agree or disagree with other things I've read?

9. What are the best ways to take notes on this?

10. What can I do to better engage with this reading? Are there great summarizing statements? What are the words I don't know? How does this reading connect with my main areas of interest?

11. If I were teaching this material to someone else, what points would I highlight? What questions would I have them wonder about? What would I want them to leave with?[4]

There is so much I appreciate about Bain's work. I first met him and read his book (very deeply, of course) when I was teaching at a small college in Ohio. I loved the idea of students gobbling up the readings and assignments I created for my classes. Bain's work not only challenges students to invest deeply in their reading, but also challenges faculty to craft classes that make space for student curiosity beyond the promise of better grades.[5]

## Mindsets Meet Reality

I confess that I also struggle with some of these ways of thinking about learning and reading in college. I long for students to be able to spend more time in deep reading than shallow and strategic reading. I also spend a lot of time with students, and, frankly, I don't think spending all our time swimming in the deep end of the reading pool is realistic.

Let's be honest, most college students do not have the time or mental energy to commit our whole selves to deep reading everything we're assigned. We have kids to get to ball games, laundry to do, and part-time, full-time, or multiple jobs to work to make the car payment, buy food, and afford tuition. While some of us head to college straight out of high school, more and more of us are coming back after having been out of the flow of school for a while. And lots of us are the first ones in our family to go to college and are just trying to figure out this whole college thing.

We should also recognize that professors and classes are very different in the amount of reading assigned. Some professors assign reasonably moderate amounts of reading and expect students to read everything deeply. Other professors will assign terrifyingly large amounts of reading and know that students will not read it all or that they'll skim for the main ideas.

This is not to say that busy college students can't do deep reading. Or that there is a right or wrong way for professors to assign readings. It's just that you need to be discerning and understand that reading is not as simple as saying, "You're in college now, so read everything deeply!" without considering these realities.

Rather than tossing out Bain's deep-reading approach altogether, I propose we adapt it. I suggest that you:

- Ask your professor or a TA about their expectations around your reading. What is it that they would like you to learn? A hint ... I'd recommend you *not* ask, "Do we need to read everything?" (This sounds like you're trying to take short-cuts.) Instead, ask, "What are the most important things you'd like for me to get out of these readings?" (This communicates that you want to focus on what is most important.)

- Make sure to always get the main ideas. This is less about asking, "What is the least amount I need to read to get by?" and more about, "What is the most important take-away in this reading?"

- Strive to read deeply, but be gracefully realistic. Don't beat yourself up if you're not spending hours reading everything.

- Consider prioritizing what you need and do not need to read deeply. You might do this by prioritizing readings in your major or main academic program. Or you might do this by watching for readings outside of your main classes that connect with your interests.

- Take excellent notes. This doesn't mean you should take mountains of notes. It means taking notes smartly. I suggest using my note-taking template (found as a free download at gutsycollege.com) to ask questions of everything you're reading. Watch for deep-reading connections across readings and classes. In a later chapter, we'll spend a whole section on the best way to take reading notes.

## A Final Reflection on Deep Reading

In wrapping up this journey through Bain's brain, there's one final note I think is important for us to remember as we think about the surface, strategic, and deep-reading approaches.

Bain argues that an important part of learning and reading begins with examining ourselves. We need to take some time to learn what motivates us. What do we care about? Beyond going to school to say we got a degree or have some new skills to get a promotion, he challenges us to consider what genuinely matters to us.

This self-examination is important because it can become a reading engagement tool. By asking how a reading connects with something we care about, we create a new way to see it. The reading moves from just words on a page to ideas that touch something that matters to us.

For instance, if you're a nursing student, reading about heart rhythms becomes more than just scribbles on a strip; it's a language you're learning to understand someone's father's health. If you're a mechanic, reading about replacing a car's head gasket becomes more than just metal and hoses; these are instructions preparing you to put your hands inside the wonder of machines. If you're a programmer, reading coding grammar becomes more than just memorizing characters; it is the language you use to create elegant compositions of logical thinking. If you can find your inspiration and weave it into your reading, the words can begin to jump off the page.

Once you've taken some time to understand what you really care about, all the other tools in this book will make more sense and become more useful. Whether you're reading an instruction manual central to your program or an academic article that doesn't catch your eye at first, there is probably something there that could matter to you. Be curious. Ask questions. Take excellent notes. Find ways to connect your reading to what matters to you. You might be surprised at what happens when you try reading deeply.

## "Take Your Life to School" Day

It was one of the most exciting Anthropology classes I'd ever taught. It wasn't because my material was better than usual or that I'd discovered some magic to keep students interested. It was thanks to Ray, Lydia, and their friends.

Ray had worked for years as a manager at a local auto-production facility. He and a few friends were finishing up their business degrees and were required to take a social science class. Lydia and several of her friends had just returned from a cross-cultural experience in India and needed the class to finish their social work majors. Instead of me lecturing and students taking notes, most of our classes turned into a big discussion about how the topics and readings helped us understand our experiences.

## Pedagogy and Andragogy

Before we get into the details of how you bring your life into your studies, let's back up a bit. In education circles you'll often hear teachers talking about "pedagogy," which typically gets used as an umbrella term for the way someone goes about teaching. In the 1950s, Malcolm Knowles, a researcher and professor of education, started asking about how well our ideas of pedagogy were serving those who come to school as adults.

He noticed that pedagogy isn't just about how one teaches, but brings with it assumptions about the way classrooms should be set up. Usually this means that an adult stands in front of the class and leads children through exercises that teach them things the teacher knows. The teacher talks and the children listen, take notes, and memorize. After all, the word *pedagogy* comes from *peda*, meaning "child," and *gogy*, meaning "to lead."

Once we begin teaching students beyond high school, Knowles argues that we need to shift our thinking and begin talking about andragogy—with the distinction of *andra* meaning "adult."[6] Knowles wanted to go beyond how to best teach children and begin thinking about the best ways to teach adults.

To be clear, this isn't just about reading difficulty. Of course, most seven-year-olds won't be able to read the sorts of things that a thirty-three-year-old can. Beyond vocabulary and grammar, Knowles points out that adults bring an entirely different purpose, interest, and set of experiences to learning and reading compared to children. Thinking about how this changes how we learn and read is generally overlooked.

While individuals can certainly be ahead or behind the developmental curve, cognitive scientists tend to mark the arrival of the "adult brain" at around age twenty-three. So, as we think about college, we'll see that most traditional college students (those who recently came from high school) are just approaching this age, and nontraditional college students (those who are coming back to college when they're a bit older) will be well beyond this age. This means that we need to pay close attention to Knowles's adult learning style since most university students are, or will soon be, entering college with an andragogical learning perspective.

What's different about learning and reading as an adult versus learning as a younger person? Knowles observed that while pedagogy tends to focus primarily on transmitting information and skills with assigned readings, quizzes, and drills that emphasize memorization, this doesn't work well with adults. Sure, we'll still be sitting through lectures and taking tests, but adults bring an accumulated wealth of perspectives, expectations, and experience to school that children do not have yet.

Knowles summarized these differences with six principles:[7]

1.  Adults are self-directed learners: their curiosity is pulled forward by their personal interests (as opposed to being directed by the interests of a teacher).

2.  Adults accumulate experience that becomes a rich resource for learning: their learning benefits from a growing pool of life experience that they bring to their learning (as opposed to a relatively shallow pool of life experience).

3.  Adults' readiness to learn is related to social roles: their interests are shaped by a multitude of relationships such as being parents, spouses, community volunteers, neighbors, employees, supervisors, etc. (as opposed to a relatively small number of social roles).

4.  Adults have a problem-centered orientation and want immediate application of knowledge: they are eager to apply their learnings to challenges and questions they are currently encountering (as opposed to gathering general information).

5.  Adults tend to be internally motivated: their motivation is fueled by personal goals or commitments (as opposed to primarily imposed upon them by parents or peers).

6.  Adults need to know the reason for learning something: they want to know why they are learning something and why it matters to them and their world (as opposed to assuming that the teacher has a good reason for teaching something).

## *So, What About Our Anthropology Class?*

You might be asking (as a good adult learner), why does any of this matter? It matters because if we want to become excellent learners and readers in college, we can use these andragogical discoveries to strengthen our reading. Rather than just reading to gather general information or collect facts that we'll use to work into a paper or hope to retain long enough to pass a midterm, we'll read with personal curiosity, life experience, and deeper questions.

Keeping Knowles's six principles in mind, we can be asking:

- "What about this reading piques my curiosity? What is interesting here?"

- "Where does my experience connect with this reading, and how does this connection help me better understand this material?"

- "How does being a parent, spouse, neighbor, community member, leader, employee, supervisor, etc. inform what I'm reading here?"

- "How does this reading suggest solutions to problems I'm facing or help me see my challenges differently?"

- "How does this reading connect with my deeper goals or things I care about?"

- "What about this reading matters to me?"

What was going on in our Anthropology class? We were experiencing the exciting engagement of andragogy. We had a diverse group of adult learners who were deeply curious about what they were reading *because* they were trying to figure out how it helped them understand their personal experiences in new ways.

For instance, Ray and his coworkers were taking the Iceberg Concept of Culture we looked at in class to examine why different departments at work had a hard time getting along.[8] Meanwhile, Lydia and her friends were taking the same concept and using it to think about how women's roles in India were different from their experience at home in Ohio. Then, the groups began sharing what they were learning and finding similarities and differences in how they applied the concept. This is what happens when thirty students bring their varied experiences and questions into a space where they are encouraged to genuinely listen and share. Fires are kindled and significant learning occurs.

## *Three Andragogy Thoughts for the Road*

In wrapping up this section, here are three hints that might help you leverage this adult learning perspective:

1. Consider adding these experiential questions to your note-taking template. We'll dig deeply into this template in Chapter 4. The one I've developed is found at gutsy-college.com with some of the questions already built in. As you read, use these questions to help better connect your experience to the text.

2. Adult learning perspectives suggest that the more experience you bring to college, the more tools you'll have to engage with your studies and reading. If you are able, seek out an internship, spend some time in a cross-cultural setting, or volunteer with an organization you're inspired by. You might also consider a gap year between your high school graduation and the beginning of college. The more experience you bring with you to your reading, the more deeply you'll be able to engage with your studies.

3. Finally, for those who are returning to college after being away for a few years, know that you are bringing with you a rich set of social connections, personal motivations, and years of perspective. Even if you might feel out of the flow of school or unfamiliar with the classroom, you bring some powerful experiences that will be uncommon among students who are fresh out of high school. The point being ... the harder you work to bring your rich experiences into class, the more deeply you'll engage with the material, and the more you'll learn. It's the formula for creating an alarmingly interesting class!

# Big Brain Learning

I've been working from home since March of 2020. Although I get to see my team as little squares on my computer screen almost every day, there are a few of them I've still never met in person. Because of this, I've learned how reliant I am on all the software I use to hold meetings, share documents, and write emails.

But when the technology doesn't work, everything comes to a screeching halt. It's in these moments that I discover how little I know about what is going on "under the hood," so to speak. This is when an emergency call to the IT department is accompanied by prayers that I'm not number 278 in the queue. I confess that while I use it a lot, I don't know much about what's going on as electrons fly around the inside of my laptop.

I have a similar sensation when thinking about how to help college students become better readers. I've learned a lot about Bloom's Taxonomy, Bain's various styles of learning, and the distinction between pedagogy and andragogy. But I still don't feel like I know what's going on inside our heads when we're reading.

Enter brain science.

Brain science looks at learning and reading from a biological and physiological perspective. In contrast to observations about learning, brain science asks what is happening as waves of electrical impulses dance through the gray matter between our ears. And how understanding these systems gives us clues into the best ways to learn and read. This isn't to say that the other reading and learning models are wrong, but that they grow out of what we notice happening when students learn. Brain science studies the impulses zinging around our heads when we read.

## *How to Best Engage Your Brain*

Brain research is still relatively young compared to the fields of psychology or education. There are lots of new discoveries being made all the time. I've picked out a short list of some of the most important discoveries that have a lot to do with how we learn and read in college. (If you want to look further into these ideas, there are some great blogs and other resources.[9]) As you read through these, think a bit about what they might mean for how you read, study, and learn:

- **Brain-based learning engages the whole body.**
  I sometimes get the impression that students think the brain is sort of like an intellectual Uber. No matter how we feel, what we've eaten, or how tired we are, we expect it to be there and ready to go at a moment's notice.

  But brain science reveals that our brain is connected to everything we are and do. Therefore, learning is strongly influenced by our stress, nutrition, sleep, and physical activity. Our brain may show up when we call it, but if we've not taken care of it, it will probably have a flat tire, unreliable GPS, and an irritable driver. If we want to become excellent readers, we need to get regular sleep, find ways to unwind, pay attention to what we're eating, and get to the gym or some regular fresh air.

- **Brain-based learning is connected to a quest for meaning.**
  Sometimes students can lose sight of why they're going to college. This is probably more of a risk for recent high school graduates than it is for students returning to the

classroom later in life because of a specific goal they have. Brain-based learning suggests that because the human experience is driven by curiosity and making connections, learning should include meaningful, rich challenges. This means that we should find ways to connect our studies and readings to things that genuinely matter to us. If we want to become excellent readers, we need to be looking for how our reading connects to why we're here in college.

• **Brain-based learning is attuned to emotions.**
Gone are the days when researchers would silo our thinking and feeling away from each other. As if our left brain and right brain are grumpy neighbors that never talk with each other. Today, most brain researchers would recognize the deep interconnection between our emotions and the way our brains work[10]. Because thinking and feeling cannot be separated, if we want to do our best reading, we should be aware of how we're feeling. Are we investing in our close relationships? Are we getting some time to care for ourselves? Are we balancing our work and our fun? If we want to become excellent readers, we need to pay attention and find ways to create supportive and energizing emotional spaces.

• **Brain-based learning recognizes two types of memory: spatial memory and rote memory.**
Spatial memory is where our brain stores routine personal experiences (like where we put our shoes, how to get to the grocery store, and the mascot of our favorite sports team). Rote memory is where we store information and facts that are mostly unrelated to everyday events,

operating as a different system and requiring intentional practice and effort to strengthen.

It turns out that learning new information becomes easier when we can connect these memory systems to each other, when we can connect facts we're trying to remember with personal experience. We can do this by finding examples in our lives that illustrate something we're reading. Or how one of our readings helps us make better sense of something we've experienced. If we want to become excellent readers, we can be looking for how our reading is connected to our lives.

- **Brain-based learning is squashed by threat.**
  Because the brain is sensitive to perceived threats (like being eaten by a mountain lion or, more likely, being embarrassed by being called on in class), the best context for learning is one of "relaxed alertness." This is where emotional safety is protected and curiosity is nurtured. This discovery encourages us to create spaces, a schedule, and regular routines that allow us to be comfortable, uninterrupted, and fully engaged in what we're doing. If we want to become excellent readers, we'll create bound-aries around our lives that allow us to read when we're awake and alert and eager to do the work.

- **Brain-based learning recognizes that each brain is unique and becomes "uniquer" with learning.**
  There was once an assumption that although children's brains were malleable and responsive to change, over

time adult brains became inflexible and unchangeable. This view has been left in the dust as researchers have found adult brains to be far more adaptable than once thought.[11] Although most people's brains have the same foundational systems, all our brains continue to become different in response to learning and experience. If brain-based learning recognizes that each brain is unique and becomes "uniquer" with learning, then it makes a lot of sense to challenge ourselves to read new things, think new thoughts, and find new ways to connect our experiences to what we're learning.

## Brain Science Takeaways

I find these brain science discoveries particularly powerful because they resonate with other perspectives on reading and learning. Where behavioral studies reveal that students who get better sleep and exercise are better able to focus, brain studies have discovered the same thing. Where learning experiments show that students who take notes learn more than by just listening to a lecture, brain studies have discovered the same thing. It means that knowing more about what's going on between our ears points to the habits that make for good readers and learners.

As we look at different reading and note-taking strategies in the next chapters, keep this brain research section in mind (so to speak!). In addition to prioritizing your health and creating spaces that foster "relaxed alertness," think about expanding your strategies in ways that engage more of your brain. Don't just take notes but ask questions about what you're reading. Begin using flash cards, write definitions, or start using mind maps in your notes. Thinking from your brain's perspective and how all those electrical impulses are whizzing around your head can give you a reading edge.

# Building on What We Know About Reading

As we reach the end of this section, I catch myself thinking, "Who would have known that so many people have spent so much time thinking about and researching what we know about reading and learning?" This chapter has walked us through a lot of what we know about reading, not just for college students, but for anyone, anywhere.

Bloom's Taxonomy provides a blueprint for the different levels of reading. It shows us that we need to start with foundational ideas and work up to more complex concepts and personal creativity. Bain's mindsets remind us that our intention matters and that genuine curiosity about what we're reading will serve us much better than just avoiding an F.

The comparison of andragogy and pedagogy helps us see that the way adults learn and read is very different from the way children do. We can use our adult experiences to invigorate our reading strategies. And our survey of brain science discoveries shows that if we want to really read and learn well, we need to also think about our emotions, stress, and other parts of our lives.

I've included these perspectives at the beginning of this book not just to fill a space or impress my colleagues. These understandings have everything to do with how we read in college. As we head into the next chapters, think about how Bloom's levels change the way you think about the classes you're taking. Ask yourself if you're bringing a shallow or deep intention to your reading. Use the andragogical principles to get a better hold on what you're studying, and use this brain science to help focus your precious time. And of course ... just keep reading. I'll show you how to do it.

CHAPTER 2

# *What We Know About Reading ... in College*

We learned some things about reading: learning and reading begins with simple ideas and becomes more complex as you get better at it and take harder classes; we can bring surface, strategic, or deep-learning approaches to our reading; there are big differences between how we think of learning for kids and for adults; and while we still have lots to learn, knowing the way our brains work can improve our reading efficiency and recall. But what should you expect when you start reading *in college*?

## *Questions About Reading in College*

When I first went to college, I remember lots of folks saying, "Ohhh, you're going to have so much to read!" and "College reading is going to be really hard!" But nobody ever told me what that really meant. I didn't know how reading in college was different from reading in high school, or the sorts of reading I did at work or at home, or how much harder it was than reading novels or emails or websites. This section is dedicated to telling you what you really need to know about reading in college.

You'll notice this section is structured as a question-and-answer session.

Here you will find answers to the seven most frequently asked questions I hear about reading in college:

1. Why should I care about the syllabus?
2. How much will I read in college?
3. How difficult will the reading be?
4. How do professors decide what to assign in college?
5. What sorts of things will I be reading in college?
6. Do I need to be a speed reader to succeed in college?
7. Do I need to read everything in college?

It's worth mentioning that what reading looks like in college can vary depending on what sort of a program you're pursuing. An English major will read different sorts of things than someone finishing out a nursing degree. Someone working on their American Sign Language certification will read different things compared to someone doing a pre-engineering degree.

While things may vary quite a bit across programs and majors, the following information is relatively consistent across schools and is a good place to begin as you think about how you're going to plan your reading and college study plans. On to the questions.

# Why Should I Care About the Syllabus?

The class syllabus is the document the professor posts online or hands out in class that outlines the class, topics, due dates for your assignments, etc. Sometimes people talk about the syllabus as the contract between you and the teacher. It explains what you're being asked to do in exchange for receiving a certain grade. Give the syllabus a thorough reading so you know what is going on. Don't be that student who asks a question to which the professor replies, "It's in the syllabus!" (BTW, professors tend to get really annoyed when students ask those questions. It shows they haven't read the syllabus the professor spent the whole summer working on! Just saying …)

When it comes to reading, the syllabus is your road map. It not only lists the books, articles, and online resources you'll be reading, but typically includes the dates for when the readings connect with the class topics. Try to finish the reading before the class that will cover this material. You might not understand it all when you're reading at first, but in that case, it will become clearer as the professor explains it in class.

The syllabus will also show you what types of readings you'll be assigned. We'll touch on the differences between textbooks and other sorts of readings in a bit. For now, know that the syllabus is your classroom GPS. Its job is to help you keep your reading on track. Thoroughly reading the syllabus and frequently referring to it is the first step in creating a great reading strategy for college.

# How Much Will I Read in College?

Before we can figure out how much you'll be reading in college, we need to understand how university courses work. Let's start with some math. A typical class load for a full-time undergraduate student is around twelve to fifteen credit hours per term or semester. This usually means taking four or five three-hour classes (or maybe some other combination that includes one- or two-hour classes). The "number-hour" means how many hours you should plan on being in the classroom or lab per week. Taking a three-hour class means that you'll spend three hours in the classroom per week (maybe one hour from 10 a.m. to 11 a.m. on Mondays, Wednesdays, and Fridays through the term or semester). Multiply this by the number of classes you're taking, and you'll find that a full-time student is in the classroom around twelve to fifteen hours per week.

Schools usually estimate that students should succeed in their courses if they study three hours outside of class for every one hour they spend in class. So, if you're in class for twelve to fifteen hours a week and then study an additional three hours for every one hour spent in class, then a full-time student should plan to spend forty-eight to sixty hours a week doing school stuff (12 to 15 in class + 36 to 45 outside of class = 48 to 60 hours per week). This is roughly the equivalent of a busy full-time job.

If you are going to school part time and taking fewer credit hours, you can tweak this formula to figure out how much time you can expect to spend in class and how much time you'll spend studying and reading. For instance, if you're taking one three-hour class, you could expect three hours in class and then nine hours of time studying outside of class. Total it up and you're up to twelve hours a week.

## *In Reality*

That is how college class time commitments are set up in an ideal world.

Now let's talk about reality.

These expectations vary a lot. Some introductory-level classes have relatively little reading, while some advanced classes have much more. Some programs are reading heavy; others are not. Some lengthy readings are easy, and some readings that are only five pages can be difficult. Some professors have high reading expectations, and others don't.

A second taste of reality is that your experience of reading in college will vary depending on how much you're reading right now. Are you a bookworm? Do you do a lot of reading for work? Do you read for fun? A recent Gallup poll shows that, in general, Americans read twelve to thirteen books a year, which is about two to three books less than five years ago.[12] While about 17% of Americans report reading no books over the past year, there is also a small group of folks who are reading a lot. My experience as a college professor suggests that if you are the sort of person who reads a lot, then the college reading load will feel less intimidating than it would for someone who doesn't read very much.

A final taste of reality is research showing that students rarely put in as many hours studying as colleges and professors expect. On average in the US, full-time students report that they typically spend about twenty-seven hours toward class and studying.[13] So, let's think about this. Say you're a full-time student taking a twelve-hour load (for instance, four three-hour classes). This means you're going to class twelve hours a week and then spending fifteen hours a week studying (12 hours in class + 15 hours studying = the 27 hours US students are reporting).

This means students are studying 1.25 hours a week for every hour in class, far less than the three hours out of class for every one hour in class that we talked about earlier. And then, of course, they wouldn't be spending all those fifteen weekly study hours reading. Some of it is spent writing papers, doing lab work, completing online postings, etc. So, according to current research, the average full-time college student might be spending six to eight hours a week reading. If you are going to school half-time or taking one class a term, this reading reality would be even less.

## So, How Much Will You Read in College?

It will vary a lot depending on your program, the complexity of your classes, and your professor's preferences. Probably more if you are full-time than if you're part-time. You'll feel it more if you're not a regular reader than if you already read a lot. And probably a lot less than your professor would like you to.

My recommendation? As you might guess, I'd love to see everyone reading a lot. But as a realist and as a former student, I get it. There's the plan, and then there's real life. Rather than using these hourly formulas as a strict law, use them as a good starting point. Then, I'd recommend being honest with yourself. What can you realistically take on? If you're juggling a full-time job and parenting, taking a full-time course load and helping the kids with homework every night, a full-time class schedule may be unrealistic. If you find yourself without many additional commitments, a full load with lots of reading is more manageable. Be honest with yourself. The more thoughtful reading you can do, the better. Take what you've learned here and be real with yourself and your family.

## How Difficult Will the Reading Be?

In the same way we learned that the amount of time you spend reading will depend on a lot of factors, your experience of the difficulty of college reading will also vary a lot. Things such as the school's academic rigor, the type of program you're in, the complexity of the classes, the professor's choices, and how much reading you're already accustomed to reading will all make a big difference.

Highly competitive schools will likely have higher expectations for their students than other colleges or universities. Nursing and medical fields will be heavy on natural sciences and mastering tons of precise anatomical and biological facts (my spouse is a nurse—one time we counted and discovered that she read about ten thousand pages during her program! Yeesh!) Students aiming for law school, engineering programs, or other advanced degrees will probably be reading more complex work.

The challenges of individual classes and professors are hard to predict. The best way to learn is probably to ask around your campus. Word of mouth will reveal the reading complexity in various classes.

And here's a good moment to think about what we learned about reading in the first section. Reading in foundational classes (*a la* Bloom's blueprint) will almost always be less diffi-cult than reading in advanced courses. Classes are designed to help you work up to more complex concepts. Also, think about Bain's challenge to read deeply. Don't shy away from hard classes. Often, the professor with the reputation of being the most difficult on campus is also the one who has the most to teach you, especially if they're teaching something you're interested in!

A little sidenote here about professors: every campus I've ever been on has one or two professors that stand out. In addition to being quirky or unusually engaging, they have two other qualities. They care deeply about teaching, and they are extremely rigorous. I remember them as the classes I was both most curious about and most terrified to enroll in. Students who take these classes often talk about them as, "Oh ... I took that one, too! It was so hard, but I'm glad I took it. Professor So-and-So was amazing!"

I would strongly encourage you to keep your ears open for these classes. Listen to what students are saying, and don't be afraid to take a class from this professor. Most students have space in their schedules to fit in some electives (courses not directly related to their major area of study) or general education requirements (sets of courses from which all students are required to take a class or two to give you a more balanced academic program). Take a class with the professor everyone says is amazing. You'll thank yourself later and have great stories to tell at alumni parties in ten years.

## *Figuring It Out*

As you can tell, figuring out how difficult reading will be at college depends on a lot of things. And there is one more way to think about reading difficulty that is useful for how we think about the complexity of college reading.

A commonly used way to assess the complexity of a reading is by using the Flesch-Kincaid readability scale. It's a simple formula that analyzes the difficulty of reading using the average number of words in a sentence and the average number of syllables in each word. More words plus more syllables equal more difficulty. In fact, you can cut and paste text into an online form, and it will analyze it and give you a reading difficulty score for that piece of writing.[14] For instance, when I entered this paragraph into the tool, it scored an 8.1. In theory, someone reading at an eighth-grade level should be able to read and understand this paragraph.

Pretty straightforward, huh? So, when you're in fourth grade, you should be reading stuff with a 4.0–4.9 reading level. In eighth grade you should be reading at an 8.0–8.9 reading level. And when you graduate from high school, you should be reading at a 12.0–12.9 reading level. Right? Ideally, yes.

## Back to Reality

Research into the reading skills of US students shows that the average reading level of high schoolers is 5.3 on the Flesch-Kincaid readability scale.[15] To put it another way … most high-school students are reading material that fifth graders should be reading. What sorts of books are at a fifth-grade reading level? Some examples include *The Hobbit* by J. R. R. Tolkien, *The Diary of a Young Girl* by Anne Frank, and *Esperanza Rising* by Pam Muñoz Ryan. To put this in a larger context, just over half of the US population between ages sixteen and seventy-four reads below a sixth-grade reading level.[16] Which also means that, on average, most US adults don't improve their reading skills between high school and later in life.

What about college? Surveys since the mid-2000s have consistently shown that the average incoming college student reads at around a seventh-grade reading level, increases their level only slightly during college, and shows little difference whether they are from a public or private school.[17] Despite professors' longing that students entering college read at a twelfth-grade reading level, research continues to show that while college students tend to have higher reading scores than the US public in general, they don't read *that* much better.[18]

## *Soooo … How Hard Is It?*

Back to our original question: how difficult will your reading be in college? Simply put, your experience with college reading difficulty will depend on a lot of things: what you're accustomed to reading right now, the school you go to, the type of academic program you're in, and the particular classes and professors you're working with. College reading will probably be more difficult than you're accustomed to, but not as bad as you might fear. The rest of this book and accompanying website will help you become an excellent reader. Don't be afraid to take the tough classes and be challenged to improve your reading. You will thank yourself for it later.

# How Do Professors Decide What to Assign in College?

Let's talk about what's going on in the heads of your professors. Once again, remember that although this captures the general idea of why professors assign reading the way they do, it will be very different from teacher to teacher, class to class, school to school, and depending on your area of study.

As you already know, college courses typically run in a series of numbers that build on each other and roughly correspond to your academic year. First-year students usually start with courses labeled as 100s, move on to 200s, and so on. If you transferred in some college credit from high school or a previous college, you may jump straight into the 200s or

300s. If you're in a two-year program, your courses will probably be in the 100s and 200s. If you're in a four-year program, your courses will run up through the 400s. If you decide to go to graduate school, the numbers will pick up again in the 500s and run up through the 600 or 700s. This is the general approach, but you'll find many schools who do things their own way.

## Back to Bloom

This is a great example of why it's good to understand a bit about Bloom's Taxonomy. Professors tend to think of 100-level courses at the foundation of that pyramid and then build later classes on top of it. So, what you're likely to find early on in your reading is a heavy emphasis on basic facts and information that fit into general frameworks and models of the field you're in. As you move beyond the Introductory 100 courses, you'll probably begin to encounter readings that argue with each other and introduce you to some of the big debates that happen in your field.

For example, in sociology, after you take Introduction to Sociology, you might move on to an Environmental Sociology course where you encounter the big debates around different ways to look at environmental issues. Environmental justice advocates look at things differently from environmental Marxists and the ecofeminist movement, and so on. The further you work your way up the pyramid, the deeper you get into specific debates and concepts.

The reason these things matter is because professors generally see 100-level courses as broad foundational courses, often called "survey" or "introductory" courses. As you work up through your courses, the classes will begin to dig deeper into specific details, and the reading will likely get more complex. Courses at the 100 level often use big thick textbooks that provide a survey of the whole field. Think "an inch deep and a mile wide" way of looking at being a physical therapist, kindergarten teacher, or accountant. You'll learn a little bit about a lot of stuff. There may be additional readings sprinkled in with the textbook, but generally they won't be too difficult.

As Bloom suggested, foundational courses are the places where you need to focus on facts, dates, and concepts. It's not that you won't be analyzing arguments or applying the material to your own experience, but this is the time to really get a good clear understanding of the field's academic landscape. This is a great place to use flash cards and mind mapping (strategies we'll look at in the next chapter).

## Building Up

As you move on to higher-level courses, you'll likely not see as many big general textbooks and will instead encounter texts, individual books, or shorter articles that focus on more specific areas. These will take something you touched on in your previous classes and push it further.

Fair warning here: there might be the same or even fewer pages to read in upper-level classes, but the difficulty can still be increasing. Again, remember this varies a lot across fields. This description is true for social science and history. Advanced English and literature courses will have you reading more difficult books. You'll probably still see big thick textbooks in chemistry, biology, and other natural sciences classes. They'll just become more specific as you move into the advanced classes. Assess these types of reading through Bloom's lens as you move through your program.

Here's another example: when I was a sociology professor, SOC 152 was our school's Introduction to Sociology course. Because it was required for many majors, about 95 percent of the students who took the class weren't necessarily going into sociology. As a professor, I needed to factor this into my reading choices for the class. I ended up choosing a big, thick sociology textbook that I thought would appeal to students with lots of different interests. I also added a contemporary academic article, bit of news, or online posting that applied the topic we were looking at. The textbook chapter was probably fifty pages and had a seventh- or eighth-grade reading level. The article varied between five and twenty pages with a highly variable reading difficulty. Maybe seventy pages of reading each week were divided between the textbook and the additional material.

Students who moved beyond this 100-level course would take classes such as Social-Psychology, Social Theory, or Environmental Sociology. These were 200- and 300-level classes. Readings often came from books that had chapters focusing on specific theories or ideas. We'd read chapters, articles, and sometimes whole books. The difficulty and quantity were both increasing. We were probably reaching tenth or twelfth grade and perhaps up to one-hundred-fifty pages a week.

Now and then I'd have an advanced senior student who would do a special study of some kind. We'd read one book every week or two. I'd also often challenge students in advanced courses to read things I thought would push them out of their comfort zone because it is good to wrestle with hard reading.

There are few hard-and-fast rules when it comes to professors' reading assignments. Most faculty have significant leeway in what they ask you to read in their classes. One of the best ways to get a sense of your professor's reading choices is to ask. Early in the term, make a quick stop by their office and ask, "What do you most hope we learn from the reading assignments?"

## What Will I Be Reading in College?

So far, we've walked through why the syllabus is so important, how much and how difficult your reading is likely to be, and what might be going on in your professor's head (that may be a scary place, so we'll not wander too far in there). Now we'll explore the types of reading you're likely to encounter.

You probably already know that there are many different genres of writing and that you read them all a bit differently. You read a tweet differently than you read a brownie recipe, a handwritten letter from your grandmother, or the new Stephen King novel. Each is set up with different purposes and is structured in different ways. You also bring different assumptions to each reading. You begin reading your email with certain expectations that are different than what you bring to that novel you just started.

In the same way, you will encounter different genres of writing in college. They, too, will have different purposes and structures, and you'll read them with different expectations. You'll encounter thick textbooks, online articles, historical fiction, biographies, blogs, videos, and so on. You probably read a variety of these materials all the time but might not think about how you read them all a little differently.

## The Six

My sense is that there are six different sorts of things you'll read in college. Chapter 3 will dig into the strategies of how to read these. For now, let's just get to know them.

1. **Textbooks:** These are those big thick books often with glossy pages and color pictures. They're often expensive if you buy them (which is why lots of students rent them now). You'll also see them in digital versions and open-source texts that you can access or download online for free. They are frequently used as the main text in what are known as introductory or survey classes, such as PSY 101 Introduction to Psychology. The reading level tends to be on the easier side. There are often vibrant illustrations

to keep students' attention since many are taking this class because it's a general education course. The ideas are clearly structured and presented in an outline form. Chapters often conclude with a concise summary and sometimes additional learning tools such as flash cards, glossaries, or test-your-knowledge quizzes.

2. **Edited Books:** These are books that include a whole variety of shorter readings often written by important scholars in a particular field. There may be ten to twelve or more readings that provide different perspectives on the topic. Each of the readings is making a particular argument (as opposed to trying to give a big overview like a textbook). Sometimes the readings are grouped together in sections because they're sort of similar. The reading level is likely more difficult than the textbook. The ideas are almost certainly built on something you learned in your survey class and are going into more detail. Professors often assign these in 200- or 300-level classes for just these reasons—they are more advanced and give you a sense of the deeper conversations in your field.

3. **Research Articles:** Almost every academic field has these sorts of readings. They're usually shorter (maybe twenty to thirty pages) and likely explore a specific topic. When I say specific, I do mean specific! These are generally written by professors, researchers, or other experts. They are written to explore a particular research question by gathering data, analyzing it, and reporting its findings. The reading level ranges from challenging to

downright cryptic. Your professor has probably read tons of these and will have likely written a few. Hopefully, they will select these because they provide deeper insight into the ideas you are exploring. They tend to be used more as you move into 300- and 400-level classes. If they fall into the areas you're really interested in, they can be fascinating. If they're outside of your interests, you might catch yourself wondering what the heck the author is trying to say.

4. **Monographs:** This is a book where a single author is laying out a well-developed vision for the argument they are making. Sometimes the book is pulling together a lifetime of research. Sometimes they have a new idea they are developing and want to share with the world. Sometimes they're responding to others they disagree with. Monographs are often several hundred pages long, and the reading difficulty can range from relatively accessible to quite challenging. They tend to have a specific focus (sort of like research articles) but are taking more time and space to develop their thoughts. Because they're longer and are building on the basics you learned in your 100 classes, most professors use them in your 200 classes and beyond.

5. **How-to Texts:** Depending on your program, you might also be reading about how to do things that are specific to your field. Nursing students will be reading about how to properly start an IV, diesel mechanics will read about how to change out glow plugs, and computer

technicians will read about how to defend against the most common phishing strategies. Professors will assign these so you can read about how to properly do something and learn some of the frequent mistakes learners can make.

The difficulty can be highly variable. If you know the field, you might find it easy; if you don't, you might feel like you're reading a foreign language. For instance, I might be able to read doctoral-level social science but would be totally lost reading an engine repair manual (thank goodness for mechanics!). Finally, these readings are often designed with action in mind. They describe the right way to do something with the expectation that a nursing student will practice hundreds of needle sticks under the eye of someone who has started thousands of them.

6. **Miscellaneous Readings:** No list would be complete without a miscellaneous category. Besides the five typical sorts of readings we looked at here, you'll encounter all sorts of things. Classes I've taught have included blogs, novels, student newspaper editorials, magazine articles, letters, films, online videos, TED Talks, and more.

   Specific academic programs will also have their unique emphases. Education programs will have you exploring different sorts of age-appropriate curriculum. Nutrition and dietetics will explore the nuances of cookbooks and recipes. Engineering, literature, and history will all have their own range of texts. Although the types I've outlined here will likely appear in all fields, you will need to regularly be asking yourself, "What sort of reading is this, and how should I best tackle it?"

# Do I Need to Be a Speed Reader to Succeed in College?

This is a question I sometimes get from students who are anxious about the college reading load. Most of the time they're not actually asking about "speed reading" per se, but are instead asking important questions about efficient reading strategies.

When most people talk about speed reading, they're imagining some magical technique that enables them to read a thousand pages in an hour or crank through Plato's *Republic* in one evening. Let's unpack this speed-reading idea a bit and get down to some useful strategies.

## *What Is Speed Reading?*

There is a lot of research out there that suggests average college students read at about two-hundred-fifty wpm (words per minute). Of course, this is dependent on things such as if you are sounding out every word, how much experience you have with reading, how accustomed you are to this particular language, and how difficult the text is. Some research suggests that people can push their reading speed up to eight hundred wpm, while others argue that anything over five hundred wpm is just skimming without much comprehension.[19] So just because you say you can tear through *Frankenstein* in one evening doesn't mean you'll remember or understand what Mary Shelley is trying to say.

## *Can I Speed Read?*

Although there are specific training programs whose techniques can significantly improve your reading speed, most of the time what people are talking about when they say "speed reading" is a more basic set of strategies that help you move through lots of words and pages faster than you probably think you could. The University of Cambridge's speed-reading site and the *Student's Guide to Speed Reading* are both great examples.[20] Neither promote a program that magically lets you read one thousand wpm. Both are full of great suggestions for how to move through your reading more quickly and with more comprehension. Because that's the point, isn't it? You can say, "I've read three hundred pages today!" but if you don't understand or can't remember it, it's all wasted time.

Genuinely useful speed-reading strategies include different techniques, such as moving away from reading every word or "hearing" each word in your head while reading, asking yourself what you really need to get out of this reading, understanding the differences among different types of texts, having a well-organized note-taking system, and spending extra time reading introductions, overviews, and conclusions.[21] The next section will dig much deeper into techniques for both reducing the time you need to spend on reading and improving your comprehension and recall.

### Do I Need to Speed Read?

So, back to our question, "Do I need to be a speed reader to succeed in college?" If you're asking, "Do I need a super-power that allows me to read five hundred pages a day?" then the answer is, absolutely not. Ninety-nine percent of my thousands of students have not been what we call "speed readers," and they did just fine with their college reading.

But if you're asking, "Do I need to think about my reading strategies and how I can improve my comprehension and efficiency?" Then yes. Many of us have not really thought about how we could speed up our reading and comprehension, or may have fallen into bad habits that can slow down our reading. Reading well in college is essential and doable. Read on to find out how.

# Do I Need to Read Everything in College?

You're pretty brave, huh? Asking a former professor if you really need to read everything in college? Two responses here: first, yeah, of course! I mean, why would professors assign it if they didn't want you to read it!? Some professors will set up reading quizzes that will test if you really read what they assigned. If you don't read, you'll lose points on those quizzes. Probably a quarter to a third of the questions on my midterm and final exams came directly from the reading. If you want these points ... then read.

Second ... I totally get it. I was a student once, too. I was also a student who had a partner and kids, and worked part time to pay for tuition, rent, and groceries. Time, money, and stress regularly piled up. All of this leaves me sympathetic toward the challenges of reality. In fact, it's one of the main reasons I wrote this book. There are a lot of things about reading that I wish folks would have told me before I started school. Not because I wanted to skimp my way through, but because I really did want to learn. I just didn't know how to get all the reading done given the busyness of the rest of my life.

The rest of this book is an answer to this question. In short, yes, you should aim to read everything you're assigned. But there are lots of different ways to read and strategies you can use to make the most of your study time.

# CHAPTER THREE

# *Setting Up to Read*

We are just about ready to look at a list of excellent reading and note-taking strategies (I'm sure you're eager to get into these). But before jumping into a list of things to do to improve your reading in college, we're going to do some setup.

Just like it's best to stretch before you go for a run or level the ground before you start building a garage, there are a few things you need to do before you open a book. Setting up is one of the most important and most overlooked steps in becoming a great college reader.

In this section I'll walk you through the five most important parts of your world to set up:

1. Setting up your mind is about being honest with yourself about heading to school. Are there things you're afraid of or nervous about? How will you handle these?

2. Setting up your schedule challenges you to take a good look at your weekly routines. Are there ways to make your life easier before classes even begin?

3. Setting up your people asks you to look around at those you are closest to. How will your college work impact them, and how can you prepare for this?

4. Setting up your space walks you through what to look for in the perfect reading spot. Where will you be able to do your best work?

5. Setting up your tech helps you look at what you need to read. What do you have, and what should you consider investing in?

Your answers to these questions and personal set-up strategies will be unique because our lives and situations are all different. Some of us are working full-time jobs and getting kids to ballgames, while others can dedicate our full attention to classwork. Some of us are retired and picking up a class for fun, and some of us are trying to shift to a new career and exploring our options.

Of course, even the most well-thought-out plans are tricky beasts. As soon as you get them organized, life throws you curveballs. And so, it's important to begin with an idea of how you are going to fit together your reading, studying, and all the rest of life while remaining flexible and willing to try new strategies.

The following five sections will walk you through these set-up plans. Some of them you might breeze through quickly, and others might take some time to figure out. Be patient and take this setup seriously. A lot of school stress comes from simply not being prepared. This section is about helping you anticipate, troubleshoot, and set up for success.

To help you think through these different parts of your life, I've also created a free downloadable workbook at gutsycollege.com. Before jumping into these next sections, hop over to the website, download the workbook, and keep it nearby. It will help you organize your life and set up your plan.

# Setting Up Your State of Mind

Have you ever felt like you don't belong in college? Maybe a sense that everyone else knows something you don't or is more ready for college than you are? Or that at any moment someone will expose you as a fraud or that somebody made a mistake somewhere and accidentally allowed you into college? This feeling is often referred to as imposter syndrome, and there are three important things to know about it as we get our minds in a place where we can read well.

## What Is Imposter ~~Syndrome~~ Phenomena?

First, although imposter syndrome can be a powerful feeling, especially for those heading to college, it isn't technically a syndrome or medical diagnosis. This is why imposter syndrome has recently begun to be labeled as "imposter phenomenon."[22]

Second, as for a definition, imposter phenomenon is the inner sense that you don't belong here, or that everyone else knows something you don't. You might have a feeling that you're faking your way along and are just waiting for someone to discover that you don't have what it takes. You might look around and think to yourself, "Why does it feel like everyone else gets it but me!?"

Third, imposter phenomenon is very real, experienced by around 70 percent of the population, is higher among folks who are in academic settings, and is even higher among students of color, first-generation students, and women in science and technology (STEM) fields.[23]

## Where Does Your Inner Imposter Come From?

There are many possible sources for each of our learned feelings of inadequacy (yes, I'm including myself here). I'm not a psychologist, so I'll not dare to dig too deeply into how we were treated by our parents, siblings, teachers, or classmates. As mentioned earlier, students of color, first-generation students, and women in STEM fields more frequently report experiencing imposter phenomena, likely because they have experienced discrimination or lacked academic mentorship from those who are familiar with the academic landscape.

In addition to childhood messages or previous academic experiences, my sense is that most folks who do even a bit of self-reflection will approach college with some trepidation. College is a space where one is judged almost daily on our performance. This pressure increases because education is so closely linked to financial and personal success in the US. The results of our academic work can feel like both a personal and professional judgment of our worth.

Sorry if this feels a little overwhelming. The main message I hope you take away here is that you can do this! Of the thousands of students I've taught and advised, I have yet to encounter a single one who could not do college work. Different things may have led them to not finish their academic program, but it was never just their abilities. At the risk of debunking a stereotype, college is less about being smart than it is about working hard, setting up your support system, reaching out when you need help, and staying the course. You are not an imposter. You might be anxious and too often compare yourself to your classmates, but don't wonder about your abilities. You can do this!

## *Seven Strategies for Overcoming Imposter Phenomenon*

As you wrestle with those imposter voices, try out these seven strategies as you head to college:[24]

1.  Connect with campus counseling or academic centers. Staff here talk with students about these feelings all the time. It's their job.

2.  Remember that your mind is connected to all the other parts of your life. Invest in good sleep, eating well, taking your medication, connecting with others, getting some exercise, and doing something fun.

3.  Seek out trusted individuals who you can share these feelings with. Think about coaches, therapists, friends,

student groups, faith leaders, friends at work, mentors, or teachers you trust.

4. Seek consistent feedback on your performance that includes recognizing your strengths.

5. Practice meditation, mindfulness, and journaling.

6. Accept that some tasks will not be done perfectly and that this is what learning is about. "Not getting it" is the first step in learning something new.

7. Review and reward yourself for progress. Overlooking success and focusing on even small mistakes feeds the imposter. Celebrating success at the end of a term or big exam is a way to remind you that you *are* succeeding.

## Seven More Hints for Battling the Imposter

In addition to these great strategies, here are seven more that I'd add. Some of them are good hints. Others just make me feel better on those days when I don't feel good enough to keep going:

1. **I'm not the only one.**
   I try to remember that I'm not the only one struggling against my inner imposter. When I look around a classroom, I remember that most everyone here is feeling the same thing. For me, this holds some community-building power. It leads me to be generous toward others in the class and be brave in asking the question everyone is

thinking but also afraid to ask (for fear of being labeled an imposter).

2. **Professors feel it, too.**

   This imposter feeling is not just for students. Where students are anxious about feeling like they don't have what it takes to do the reading or write the paper, professors are anxious about getting their work published, getting good teaching reviews, and impressing the department chair or academic dean.

3. **Imposter = success?**

   Paradoxically, the imposter phenomenon that can make you think you can't be a success in college tends to more frequently strike those with high-achievement personality traits. So, if you find yourself feeling like an imposter, you may be among the most prepared to do well in college. Weird, I know.

4. **Manage; don't conquer.**

   My personal experience is that the imposter phenomena is not something we expel from our lives like having an appendix removed. It's more about managing the struggle like a recovering alcoholic. As we face new challenges, more difficult readings and projects, advanced concepts, and more complicated skills, most of us may return to a sense of "now they'll discover that I can't do this!" It's important to think of this personal challenge as one that is never completed. We just get better at recognizing it, responding to it in healthy ways, and moving forward.

5. **Use your strengths to help you move through the challenge.**

   Say you're in a nursing program and are anxious about learning how to place a central IV line. You're convinced that you're the only one who is going to foul it up, and you get nervous when everyone is watching you. But you also know that lots of practice makes you more comfortable with what you're doing. So … before going to class, find a way to practice your IV sticks, all by yourself, a lot. Maybe on an orange or grapefruit rather than your roommate or cat (well, depending on how you're feeling about your roommate or cat). If you know that solitary preparation makes you more comfortable in front of a group, use what you've learned about yourself.

6. **Just do it.**

   Some folks who get caught in the imposer trap have strong perfectionistic tendencies that can keep them from taking the next step until they think all the pieces of the puzzle are in place. Unfortunately, that perfect preparation rarely happens. Rather than wait forever, get things as lined up as possible, then go.

7. **Ease into the adventure.**

   Other folks feel like they don't need to prepare; they just need to jump. But going to college full time can be an expensive and time-consuming change that affects you and everyone around you. Rather than quitting your job and going to college full time, maybe just take one class to test things out. See what works and what doesn't. Get a feel for the academic world. Try out new reading and note-taking strategies. See how class time fits into your family and life. Afterwards, stand back and ask yourself how it felt. How did you deal with your imposter threats? What is the right pace for your college path?

Setting up your state of mind is about being honest with yourself about yourself. It's about being willing to connect with others and share what you're experiencing. Once you begin to see that others are probably feeling the same way, you can give yourself and others the grace to do your best and discover it is more than enough to succeed. Use the strategies found here and know that you are more than good enough to be a success in college!

# Setting Up Your Schedule

One of my earliest school day memories was shopping for supplies. It was one of the few bright spots in the late summer when my friends and I saw our vacation days dwindling. I still love shopping for school supplies. Weird though it may be, wandering the aisles or scrolling online through the neon highlighters, colored pens, mechanical pencils, and planners of every imaginable sort still gives me a creative rush.

Even if you don't share my unhealthy obsession with school supplies, one of the most important steps in succeeding with your reading in college is setting up your schedule. If you've already got a well-organized routine, it's still worth your time to stand back and ask how well your schoolwork fits into the rest of your life. In this section we'll look at how much time you'll spend studying and some practical steps for fitting it in.

## How Much Time Will You Study?

How are you going to fit your class attendance and reading time into the rest of your life? Rather than signing up for a class and hoping for the best, it's worth asking how you are actually going to do it. I'd recommend using the one hour in class to three hours of studying formula we looked at earlier as a good starting point. I'd also remember that reading and study time vary from person to person.

You might even create a simple strategy for tracking this. As you begin your classes, jot a note (maybe in the top corner of your notes, highlighted, or using a bright purple pen?) indicating how long it took you to read the material for this class today or this week. As you move through your classes, you'll begin to see how much time you actually use. You might even notice that it takes you longer to get through your reading when you're with friends or after 9 p.m. than it does working on your own at 10 a.m. Use this to decide how long you need to block out for reading and the best time to do it.

I'd encourage you to be creative here. There are many spaces in our days that disappear into doomscrolling or watching videos. Reclaiming even a little bit of this time can give you the space you need to add that reading to your schedule. For me, I'm really tempted to get lost in social media after 8 p.m. I'm learning to catch myself and grab a book rather than spiraling down a social media rabbit hole. The important point is, take some time to think through your schedule. Everyone's experience is a bit different, which is why it's important to monitor yourself and adjust based on what suits your life.

## *Your Personal Reality*

If we're not honest with ourselves, great plans fall apart the minute they touch our personal reality. It is essential that you be honest when it comes to going to college. This starts with asking yourself what you can realistically accomplish. You might admire those folks who tell stories about being a single parent, raising three kids while working a full-time job, and going to medical school, but there's usually more to those stories than you hear about.

As for your personal routine ... is it going to be as simple as giving up your evenings binging your favorite series to read more? Or will you need to take a book with you to the kids' basketball practices? Will you need to talk with your employer about shifting your work schedule around a bit so you can get to class in the afternoon? Maybe you can flex your time and work a bit more Monday through Thursday so that you can go to class and read on Fridays? Maybe you take a bit longer lunch so you can get an additional thirty minutes of reading in every day?

Even if you're an eighteen-year-old full-time college student without kids and other big bills to pay, you still need to think about this. I remember tutoring some student athletes whose daily calendars ran from 5 a.m. to 10 p.m. every day. You'll likely have a part-time job or internship to work around. And don't forget the clubs and leadership groups you're getting connected to. No matter where you're at in life, when you're taking college classes, it pays to take a close look at your schedule.

## *Selecting a Planner*

A class planner with a calendar is one of the most helpful college tools. If you've never used a planner, no problem. We're going to walk through how to use it. If you've already got a system you like, that's great. This is the time to ask yourself how well it's working and if there are changes you need to make.

So, what is a planner? It is a paper notebook or digital application that you enter dates and events into to keep track of all the assignments that will come at you during college. They're usually a combination of pre-printed daily, weekly, or monthly calendars with spaces for to-do lists. They come in all sizes and prices, and are usually set up either by a calendar year (January through December) or an academic year (September through August).

Useful planners are ones that have enough space for you to enter school and personal events. As you build your routine using your planner, you will reduce your cognitive load (a good expression to look up—a fancy word for the mountain of things we all need to keep in mind just to move through life) and reduce the chances you'll forget an exam date. Good planners, like automatic payments to and from your checking account, are tools to make your life easier.

## *Types of Planners*

What sort of planner should you use? Some folks like paper notebooks because they're more tangible and just feel good to lay open on your desk. You can use different colored pens for different classes. Use highlighters or sticky notes for special reminders. Opening a planner in front of you on your desk gives you a single snapshot of your weekly or monthly plans. If you're looking for some good examples of paper planners, check out this helpful guide that reviews a dozen different styles you might consider.[25]

A close cousin of this notebook is a paper or erasable calendar you can hang on your wall. I've sometimes used these as ways to organize large projects where I need to plan projects six or twelve months out. Unlike planner notebooks, these large calendars will let you see many months at one time. Not very compact, but great for long-range planning. I've used At-a-Glance calendars with success.[26]

Other people like apps because if you're carrying around a phone, tablet, or computer anyway, why not keep your planner on there, too? One useful advantage of apps over paper planners is that you can set recurring dates (for example, these are nice for entering those classes that meet three times a week, every week) and special reminders for when projects are due.

Many computers and widely used platforms (e.g., Microsoft, Apple) have calendar systems built into them. These might work well for you. If you're looking for something specific to academic planning, there are lots of options. Some are free; others have monthly or one-time fees. If you're looking for some good examples of apps, calendy shares some of the most popular options at this site.[27]

## Using a Planner

Now that you've found the perfect planner (or something you're willing to give a try), how do you use it? You might think that all you need to do is start filling it with dates. You can surely do that, but before you begin filling it up, read through these suggestions.

I recommend you do four things:

1. Add all the times for classes, work, basketball practice, dinner with the family, holiday breaks, kids' birthday parties, etc., that you can think of. You want to anchor your schedule with events that are set and won't move. Create a color scheme for these (yay, colored markers!). Put family in one color, gym workouts in another color, and maybe each class you're taking gets its own color, too. The idea here is to create a solid skeleton of your schedule that you will fill out.

2. Add all the due dates for your class projects. This is where you make good use of the class syllabus. Most professors follow the syllabus very closely. Note all the papers,

exams, online postings, group presentations, and other dates found there. As you do this, you will begin to get a feel for pinch points (aka places in your life where things might start to look pretty busy). That's okay. In a bit we'll see how to use your planner to contend with these.

3.  Look at your major assignments and projects and break them down into smaller pieces and backward plan them. This strategy is called backward planning because you're going to set a goal that is in the future and then work backwards to today with small steps to accomplish it without panicking.

    For example, say you have a paper due on Monday the 25th. It's a comparison of how two different historians explained the beginning of the US Civil War. The paper is required to be five pages long, and it needs to include at least three academic sources (i.e., not Wikipedia or *People* magazine). Because today is the 4th, you have about three weeks before it's due. So, in your planner, you're going to note that this week you will find your three resources, read and take notes on them, and create a very rough outline. Next week you write down that you're going to develop the outline and complete a draft of the paper. The final week you'll revise the paper, add your conclusion and introduction, and turn it in. Bingo, baby! No all-nighters required!

4.  This is the time to use your planner not to cram, but to anticipate. For instance, if you know you've got a

birthday party coming up this weekend and a midterm on Monday, this is the week to put in a bit more study time on Thursday and Friday knowing that it is going to be difficult to do much reading this weekend. Likewise, as you fill in your planner, you will discover times in the year where projects and exams pile up (often toward the middle and end of a term or semester). Since you can control when you finish a paper but cannot change the date of a test, you can make your life easier by using a planner to recognize this, finish projects early, and create space for you to prepare for exams.

## *Your Calendar and the Rest of Life*

Something to keep in mind as you're building your calendar is the connection between rest and reading. Believe it or not, reading is hard work. Studying hard for a day can leave you as mentally exhausted as your muscles after a day of hard physical labor.[28] Taking regular breaks from your reading, getting some fresh air, aiming for a consistent seven to nine hours of sleep, and working some other self-care routines into your schedule will make a big difference in your ability to read. Do not trade rest for more reading time.[29] Find a way to do both.

Remember, too, that there is a social dimension to this formula. You need to talk with your family and friends about this. It's important to be aware that your friends and family have a huge impact on your success in school. It is worth taking the time to talk about your schedule and how you need to organize your life to accomplish this exciting goal.

## *Revisit, Review, Revamp*

When you get to the end of the term, do two things. First, celebrate your victories. Your calendar is probably piled high with due dates and accomplishments checked off your lists. Congratulations! It is amazing how much you accomplished over the past three months or so!

Then, ask yourself what worked and didn't work with your calendar. Not just studying and reading, but the rest of life. You thought you were a night owl, but you noticed that after 10 p.m. your brain sort of shuts down. Or you noticed that you thought you could get some reading in while watching your daughter's swim practice but discovered that you really ended up talking with all the other parents. Maybe you noticed that when you're in a regular walking or workout routine, everything feels a bit better. Maybe your time at the gym is a great time to listen to the novels you don't have time to sit and read anymore. As you look back over these past few months, what do you notice? What do you want to keep, and what can you tweak and improve?

After some review, I'd recommend taking the top two or three things you've thought about and do some genuine redesigning. Don't try to change everything. Talk with your family about redividing up the chores. Talk with your friends about better times of day for you to study. Work in a trip to the gym three or four times a week. Then implement them for next time. If you do this a few times, you will not only create a system that will get you through school but may well have created a tool you can use to help maintain some balance for the rest of your life.

## Setting Up Your People

This is one of the most important and overlooked reading preparation steps. As we learned already, the emotional and social parts of our brain are intimately connected to our learning centers. So, if you want to read well, you need to take your people seriously. You may be the one going to school, but it impacts everyone around you.

Think about it:

- Going to school will change the way you spend time with your current friends, how often you'll see them, and the sorts of things you'll do together.

- Going to school will introduce you to new people who share your interests in new ways, which will lead you to doing new things together.

- Going to school will change how you and your family plan for who is working, how many hours, and how much money you need to pay bills.

- Going to school will change your and your family's routines and rhythms: who makes dinner, who gets the kids to activities, how you do vacations, and what your evenings and weekends look like.

- Going to school will change the sorts of stresses you and your family face and will challenge you to find new ways to face these together.

Sound daunting? Well, maybe. But getting your people together as you head to school can also be a transformative moment for everyone. It's an opportunity to bring your team together around a common goal, learn how to be flexible, find new ways to listen to each other, and discover that your group chemistry makes you more than the sum of each person's parts. If you have kids, it's a great way to model how a family works together to support each other's life dreams! The key to making this transformative turn is intentionally figuring it out together.

## How to Get Started

I suggest six steps to begin:

1.  Make a list of those who are most likely to be impacted by your heading to school. This may include your closest friends, parents, partner, kids, and others around you who come to mind. I suspect you've already done a bit of this as you've begun making plans to go to school.

2.  Make an intentional point of sitting down with these people and talk about how going to college will change your routines. It is easy to assume that your plans won't affect them much (they will!) and that they'll have figured out your plans on their own (they won't!). They will probably appreciate your effort to communicate clearly.

3. What to talk about? Of course, this is going to be very different depending on who you're talking with. You don't have the same relationship with your high-school friends or parents in the same way you are part of the lives of your kids or you show up to work with your boss. Remember, too, that this is a two-way street. There are some things you're going to need (e.g., time to read in the evenings). There are also some things your people are going to need (e.g., making sure the kids still get to school in the morning). Here's a quick list of things you might consider talking about:

   - What are the chores around your house that you'll need to rearrange or share in new ways?

   - How will you reorganize your budget to adapt to these changes?

   - Do you need to talk with your employer about changing your work schedule?

   - Are there changes in your daily or weekly schedule or responsibilities that will impact your family's routine?

4. Create some understandings. As your conversations begin to reveal some changes in routines and responsibilities, write these out. No need to get this notarized or put it into a spreadsheet (unless you're into that sort of thing), but it is a great idea to at least jot down the changes you are planning. Doing this forces you to get specific (like who's going to take out the trash and do the dishes). It's

also a good reminder about what you all agreed to. Need some additional ideas? In the endnotes you'll find a great template from the University of Florida for roommates in a dorm.[30] And a slightly different format for folks sharing an apartment.[31]

5. Be responsible. In other words … do your part. If you agreed to something, make sure to do it. Yes, you're going to school and have new responsibilities there. But you are also part of a bigger team. They need you to do your part in the same way you need them to do theirs.

6. Revisit and revise. Make sure to look over and tweak these understandings together. Sometimes that might happen spontaneously when a change in your life some-where requires you all to do some rearranging. You might also look at these plans at the end of a term or semester when your class schedule changes, or if you have kids, when their school schedule changes.

Heading back to school is both an invigorating and challenging move. Making a point of including the people around you, being honest about what you need from them, listening carefully about what they need from you, and committing to making this an adventure that everyone is working together for can become a transformative opportunity beyond your learning.

# Setting Up Your Space

Location, location, location. In the day of brick-and-mortar stores, this was all about putting your shop somewhere where everyone would walk by, stop in, and buy your stuff. In the day of online shopping, location, location, location still applies, but it's in the form of how to get thousands of retweets or how to optimize your search engine results.

When heading off to college, we're usually not encouraged to think about our location quite as much. But setting up your space is an essential step in succeeding with your reading. In this section we'll walk through the elements of a perfect study space, some suggestions for where you might look for good places to work, and a few reflections for the road.

## Questions to Ask Yourself

What do you need to create the perfect location? Here are seven questions you can ask yourself when you're looking for a great place to read.

1.  Is it accessible? Your home, dorm, or apartment is prob-
    ably the most accessible to you, but as the following
    questions will reveal, it might not be the best place to
    read. Still, your study location needs to be close enough
    so that you're not spending more time getting there
    than doing your work. It might be near your home, near
    your classes, near your work, or on your regular paths
    between them.

2.  Is it comfortable? As you might guess, this can be a bit tricky. You want to be somewhere that's not too hot, too cold, too windy, and so on. On the other hand, falling asleep in that comfy chair in front of a big sunny library window isn't very helpful. Look for comfortable but not nap-inducing.

3.  Is it equipped? Do you need coffee or tea to study? Does the place have Wi-Fi if you need to get online? Or could you maybe just use your phone's hotspot? Do you need a table to spread your notes and books on? Do you have access to a bathroom? Are there convenient charging outlets for your gear? And a pretty obvious one: is it open when you need it to be?

4.  Can you concentrate here? How noisy is it? Are there TVs on every wall? Is there a band in the corner? Is it too busy? Is it too quiet? Are you too cloistered? Is there too much to look at? Are the baristas glaring at you because you only ordered an ice water and have been sitting at that same table for four hours? The best way to judge this is to try it out and see what happens. Are you able to work here or not?

5.  What are you going to work on here? There are some spaces that work great for reading but are terrible places for writing papers. Some places make great group study spots but would never work for solo concentration. You might end up discovering different places for different sorts of studying.

6. What's it going to cost you? Libraries, parks, open buildings on campus, and staying at home are generally free. Renting a co-op office space can run you $300 a month. Cafés don't always smile at you coming in with your protein bar in search of free Wi-Fi. If you're a fan of coffee shops, keep three things in mind: first, you ought to buy something (a $3 coffee will generally buy you several hours of freedom from baristas sneering at you). Second, coffee shops near campus are accustomed to students hunting for study spots and are often lenient about you camping and writing a paper all afternoon. And third, don't forget parking. If you drive, is it free or will it cost you? If you're feeding a meter, will you need to pack up every two hours, walk down, pay the parking meter, and then walk back? (Do I sound grumpy, like I've had to do this lots of times? Yes, I have. It's a big hassle.)

7. Finally, what time of day do you need the space? Some spaces work great in the morning (for instance, working at home when the kids are at school) and terrible in the evening (as in when the kids are home from school). A coffee shop may be great in the afternoon when everyone is in class, but not in the evening when the local band is playing. Think about how your sense of a good place to study changes depending on the time of day you need it.

## The Options

Now that we've walked through the elements that make for a great study space, here's a list of ideas for places you might consider. As you read, you'll probably begin thinking of options in your world. Jot these down and think of the pros and cons of each. You might also check out the free downloadable workbook at gutsycollege.com. It includes pages that help you think through the best places to study.

- **Home:** We'll start here because it's pretty obvious. Your house, dorm, or apartment can be a great place to work since you won't need to drive there and have access to a bathroom or places to charge your equipment and can probably spread out your books and papers. But of course, working at home can be tricky. It can be easy to lie down on your bed for a quick study break and wake up two hours later. Sometimes the kids need a snack, your roommate barges in, the laundry is begging to be folded, or you'll say to yourself that you'll only play fifteen minutes of video games as a quick break (yeah, right)!

- **Campus or public library:** A great option. Since this is where many people come to study when not at home, there are usually open tables, bathrooms, Wi-Fi, and charging stations. Lots of libraries have quiet study rooms (that you might need to reserve). Many will let you bring in your own drinks if they're in sealed containers (great if you need coffee or tea to keep you going and don't want to pay for it).

- **Empty classrooms and open public buildings:** You'll need to search around a bit for these, but many campuses have spaces that are wide open and set up with study areas. Check out different buildings around campus. Some campuses are so expansive that there are buildings you may have never been in. As you explore, you may encounter administrative staff who oversee the space. Don't feel shy to ask them if it's okay if you study there. You might be surprised to find a little corner somewhere that hardly anyone knows about or uses. It could become your favorite reading hangout.

- **Coffee shops:** Confession ... these are my personal favorite. But like all these options, there are pros and cons. Many coffee shops in college towns are accustomed to students coming in to study. Yes, you'll probably need to buy something, but for me, the reduction of distractions is worth it. You're probably on a budget, so try to resist the venti double soy hazelnut vanilla cinnamon white mocha with extra white mocha and caramel (at least don't order it every time you visit). Think, too, about how well this space fits into the flow of your day. Are there some times of day that work better than others? Can you genuinely concentrate here?

- **Cafeteria over lunch:** Whether you actually eat in a cafeteria or are just stopping to dig into your sack lunch, this can be a good place to work. Pull out a book or just review and tune up your calendar. I've also used it as a place to download class slides or search for class materials that I'll use for later. In general, I've found lunch a poor time to concentrate on something but a good time to organize and clean up my calendar and notes.

- **Friends' or relatives' homes/apartments:** Probably not one you've thought about, but they can be a pretty good option if available. I had a friend whose grandmother lived in town but was out running errands almost every afternoon of the week. He worked out a deal where he could go to her house to study in the afternoons. It had everything he needed for free. Do you have family or friends around with whom you could work out a deal?

- **Your car:** Another less considered option, and honestly, I've never made this work. But maybe you can. It may be a bit tight, but if you need to listen to a podcast for class or have some time in between other things, it can be a good place to read. I've never quite been able to figure out how to set up a laptop to write a paper in the car, but if you're just reading, it can work.

- **Kids' activities:** Another one I've never been able to make work, but I've seen others who can. Again, probably not the place to write a paper, but if you need to read, it might be fine. My problem is that I'd prefer to watch my kids or talk with nearby parents rather than do homework. My suggestion ... rather than trying to multitask, just enjoy your kids. Then go home and do your homework.

- **Outdoors:** This option is seasonal and, again, depends on what works for you and what you're trying to get done. I've taken a folding chair to a park and have gotten quite a bit of reading done. My challenge is that I tend to zone out and enjoy the breeze and listening to the leaves way more than reading. I experience working outdoors like studying at my kids' activities. I need to choose one or the other rather than trying to do both at once. But again … you do you.

## More Tips

Before we move on, a few thoughts for the road. Again, use what works for you.

- **Relaxed alertness:** At the beginning of this book, we discovered in the brain science section that the ideal learning frame of mind is what we call "relaxed alertness." In other words, a space where you can relax in a way that allows you to concentrate. Not "relaxed drowsiness" where you're dozing off, or "anxious alertness" where you're reading but mentally looking over your shoulder for the next social media post or childcare crisis. Relaxed alertness is a thoughtful centeredness that allows you to genuinely focus on what you're reading. When looking for the best places to study, ask yourself, "Can I be relaxed and alert here?"

- **Know yourself:** What works for you? For example, for me, a noisy coffee house is one of the very best places for me to focus and read deeply. Music can be blasting, the folks at the table next door might be cackling, and the baristas are laughing and taking orders. It all just becomes blissful white noise that whisks away my distracting mental chatter. You may resonate with this or think I'm weird. No worries, I'm cool with that. Are there places or times you should or should not read because of what you've learned about yourself?

- **Trial and error:** It doesn't hurt to mix things up a bit. One of the best ways to decide if a space works for you is to go there and try it out. You'll quickly learn which spaces support your reading and which get in the way.

- **Best friends or worst enemies?** Think carefully about how you're going to include your friends in your reading plans. While the suggestion "Hey, we should get pizza and study together tonight!" might sound like a great idea, a lot of the time there's way more pizza than there is studying. I'm not saying don't study with your friends. I'm just saying think about what really works. Once again, I wonder if it works better to just go and enjoy hanging out with your friends without studying, and then block out some other time on your own to get your reading done.

- **Keep an inventory:** After a few classes, I started to build a mental inventory of reading and study spaces. I'll often scroll through them in the morning when thinking about which is going to work best for that day. What is your list? What are the pros and cons for each?

Succeeding in college takes more than just finding the best spaces to study. Finding a great reading spot isn't everything, but the right space is an important part of the formula for success. Whether you're selling gasoline, scouting music video spots, or finding a place to read, you need to ask,

"Where are the places that let me get work done?" Location, location, location!

# Setting Up Your Tech

Technology has become so much a part of our lives that it's easy to not even think about it. But when you're entering college, it's worth taking some time to figure out how to set up your technological world.

This section looks at the most common college technology needs. We'll review current thinking about the types of media that work best for reading and walk through a list of tech, broadly speaking, that you'll likely need for college. Mind you, I'll not be making suggestions for exactly what computer to buy or headphones to use. You probably already have your preferences, and any suggestions I'd have will be out of date twenty-four hours from now. If you'd like specific suggestions, do a search for "reviews best (whatever)" and begin skimming. You will quickly see some items appearing toward the top of most lists.

## *A Sidenote*

Reading technology is complicated. Gone are the days when we assumed that we'd always be reading from paper pages bound together as a book or printed out and stapled at the corner. As you well know, in addition to old-school paper, reading media ranges from laptop screens and computer monitors to tablets, phones, and audiobooks.

Today's challenge is even more complicated than simply choosing one reading option and sticking with it. You will be juggling several of these options simultaneously in each of your classes. You might be reading from a paper text-book, downloading articles from the library's digital indices, watching a video, and taking notes on paper or a tablet, and then filing digital copies in folders in your computer that are being backed up to a campus network or the cloud. And we've only seen the beginning impacts of artificial intelligence on all of this.

For some, this juggling might be second nature. If you've grown up accustomed to these interactive acrobatics, you might read this and think, "Meh … what's new?" For others, this technological landscape may feel as if you've been dropped into a digital *Hunger Games*. In either case, this tech setup section walks you through the key questions to ask yourself. Even if you feel like your tech is put together, you can use these ideas to double-check your plans.

Before taking an in-depth look at some equipment you'll need to consider for college, let's take a minute to look at how different sorts of media influence your reading.

Here are a few questions that many ask about technology and reading:

- **Is it better to read a paper book or a digital version?**
  Evidence seems to be mounting that paper is better for reading than screens.[32] Although we're not exactly sure

why this is, it might be due to eyes getting tired of screen flicker or the risk of being distracted with notifications popping up while you're reading. Because screens are less oriented to a static page, our brains may have a harder time spatially orienting our reading to a specific location on the page, which makes recall more difficult. If you read more from screens than paper, make sure to mute your notifications and give your eyes an occasional break.

- **If you're going digital, is it better to read from a phone, tablet, or computer screen?**
  This is mostly a function of personal preference and ease of access. Phones are great for portability and audio books, but some texts will be almost impossible to read on a phone because of their font size. A laptop will give you more screen space but may be a bit harder to lug around. Tablets can be a good compromise but can still be too small to read some articles or take notes. This is encouragement to think about what tech to use for which purpose. When does it make sense in your routine to use your phone versus a tablet versus a computer?

- **Is it better to read or to listen to an audio book?**
  The jury is still out on this one.[33] You might think of it this way … reading and listening are two different ways to engage the same text. It's sort of like the difference between reading the book and watching the movie. There are pros and cons to each method. Reading is more active, easier to pace, and easier to take notes on. Listening can be done while at the gym or driving kids to school but is

more passive and harder to take notes on. You might think about which sorts of material work better for reading or listening. Which do you need to take notes on, and which can you sort of breeze through? And then, where and when does it make sense to do either of these?

The key here is to think about what you're reading, your resources, and how these options will fit into your routine. I remember getting some great audiobook reading done while walking from my car to campus. It will be different for everyone. Some careful thought here can pay dividends later.

## Your Technology Options

On to some technology suggestions. Here we'll walk through the sorts of tools you should consider when starting your college classes. If you've not done it already, this would be a good moment to download the workbook from gutsycollege.com. It contains a section where you can record your responses to these questions and think through your technology needs.

## Biotech

This may sound a little sci-fi-ish, but just roll with me here. Despite futurist warnings about computer chips in our brains, there are lots of ways we already supplement our daily living with technology. The two that have the greatest impact on our reading are our eyes and ears. Before we get into computers and other reading tools, it's important to do a system check on your own biotech.

- **Your Eyes**

  I don't know when you've last had your eyes examined, but a trip to the eye doctor is worth it. If you're one of those who want to hold onto the idea that no matter how old you are, your eyesight is just fine, it's time to swallow your pride. There's no shame in taking care of yourself. Reading makes your eyes work hard. An eye exam and possibly picking up some reading glasses or getting an adjustment to your contacts or eyeglass prescription will save you some serious headaches.

- **Your Ears**

  In the same way you take care of your eyes, make sure to take care of your ears. You should seek out a medical professional if you experience hearing loss, sinus pain, ongoing nasal congestion, sore throat, or ringing in your ears.[34] Besides making sure you keep your ears healthy, you might consider keeping some headphones or earbuds around to dampen the noise you'll inevitably face wherever you're reading. Choose music or rainforest sounds that become white noise for you. If you can splurge for it, noise-canceling technology is amazing. A decent set of headphones can turn a distracting space into an excellent study spot.

- **Additional Support**

  Most campuses have offices and specific supports dedicated to helping students with physical, intellectual, and other challenges to their success in college. Most professors will reference the campus Disability Services in their syllabus. I strongly encourage you to visit this office, if for no other reason than to find out if you are eligible for support. In my experience, students are embarrassed to admit they could use some support. Be brave. Get want you need and help normalize the fact that there is nothing wrong with asking for help. Go visit them.

## Low Tech

There are a whole variety of less digital tech that you need for class (we're not quite to computers, tablets, and other gadgets yet). These are items we often use but don't think about. These are also items that make a huge difference in our productivity. Some of these you'll have already, and others you might never have thought about. Read (deeply of course) though this list, and make a list of new things to pick up or tweaks you need to make to your current system.

- **Kitchen table, chair, footrest, sitting bike, or standing desk?**
  You need some basic equipment that lets you position things so you can work on them. Recliners might be good for reading (and sleeping?), but you'll need a table or desk for other sorts of reading, writing, and spreading out your materials. There are tons of desk and chair accessories out there. I'd recommend trying a few different things. Keep an eye out for equipment that genuinely supports your health and reading (as opposed to investing your school loans into the latest craze).

- **Lighting**
  Something to test out. Are you working by a window or cloistered in a room? Do you prefer warm or cool light?

I've come to really like bouncing light off a nearby wall rather than blasting a bulb down onto my page. I often look for alternatives to fluorescent lights as these seem to suck the life from my soul.

- **Backpack**

  Even though electronic texts are beginning to replace hard copies, you'll still be carrying around some books and other gear. I'd recommend finding a pack big enough to have a sleeve for your electronics and a couple of pockets for water and other supplies. More than a basic one-pocket bag but less than a three-month Appalachian Trail hiking backpack.

- **Library Card and Online E-book Borrowing Registration**

  You can save big money by borrowing or renting books instead of buying them (especially if they are books outside your main area of study). Many libraries belong to electronic borrowing networks that give you access to millions of texts. Your campus library will be the place to begin, but don't underestimate your local public library.

- **Pens, Pencils, Paper, Highlighters, Etc.**

  You do you. I confess that I love buying school supplies and am *very* particular about the pens and pencils I use (even if I don't use them much anymore). For me, a trip to get my school supplies at the beginning of each semester is a ritual that signals the beginning of a new set of classes. Keep a few of these in your pack.

- **Water and Snacks**

  More good things to include in your backpack. Water (or coffee) is a must for me. As is a small bag of trail mix and a protein bar. When I need to stay late or miss lunch, I'm always thankful to discover these in my backpack. You don't need a gourmet meal, but you'll thank yourself for having a little fuel on an unexpectedly long day.

- **Medical and Personal Supplies**

  Take a few minutes to think about what you'd like to have on hand for surprises or emergencies. I had a little pull-string bag with some of my medications, gum, fingernail clippers (I'm trying to kick my nail-biting habit), and a few other things. Like your snacks, you'll be glad to find them when you need them.

- **Sweater or Sweatshirt**

  Again, you do you. I am frequently surprised by how much the temperature can vary from room to room or building to building on campus. I typically keep a warm pullover in my backpack for the occasions when the AC is on over-drive in the summer or when someone forgot to reset the thermostat on that first freezing day in winter.

## High Tech

And finally, there's your high-technology world. This is all that digital tech that has become essential for college. Although you can certainly take notes in spiral-bound paper notebooks, most classes now require that you access assignments and digital readings from online library indices.

I do think it is possible to do your college work without owning your own computer. But today, having your own makes a lot of sense. Besides there being some very reasonably priced computers out there that provide word-processing and internet-browsing capabilities, there are some financial advantages to being a student when it comes to purchasing a computer for school.

Here are some of the key questions to ask yourself before investing in high tech for college:

- **Books, Tablets, or Computers?**
  Consider how you think you'll be doing most of your reading. Will you be reading paperback books, rented texts, or mostly digital versions? You should probably count on some of each. In this case you'll probably need a decent tablet or laptop. I recommend avoiding desktop systems for school. Today's laptops have just as much processing muscle as most desktops and are far more portable.

- **How Much Should You Spend?**
  My suggestion: get the best you can reasonably afford. Technology goes out of date quickly. If you buy something several years old already, you might only have a couple of years of use before needing to upgrade. Students can often get a discount on computers used for class. Consider that the discount might make it a good time to buy.

- **Before You Buy**
  Note that some schools allow you to add the purchase of a computer to your financial aid package. This might

or might not be a good idea for you. Weigh the pros and cons before putting another $1,000 to $2,000 into school loans. Also, if you're considering purchasing some new technology, you might consider waiting until classes are about to start to drop that big money. At the very least, contact the school or program to find out what they'd recommend. Some schools or academic programs have very particular technology recommendations. You'll want to follow these in case there are specific software requirements associated with your classes.

- **Taking Notes**
  You'll want to think about your note-taking plans. Some students use paper notebooks, others type in class, and others use digital tablets. I frequently see students using a laptop to read and take notes at the same time. This can be difficult to do on your phone. Thinking about how you want to take notes might influence your tech decisions.

## Software

Software falls under high tech, but it is also a world unto itself. New apps and programs are exploding onto the scene every day. Here are some software-related items to think about. These are all related to your reading routine in one way or another. Some of them you may be aware of, while you may have never heard of others. Consider what you've got and what you need to add to your toolbox.

- **A Reference-organizing Tool**
  These are programs where you can enter a reading's title, date, author, etc., into a library that allows you to create bibliographies and resource lists in a snap. Some common ones include Zotero, Mendeley, and Endnote. Over many years of studying and teaching I've entered thousands of references into my system. Now when I need a citation, I just find it, click it, and there it is! With a click of a button these reference programs will reformat your endnotes, footnotes, or bibliography from APA to MLA to Chicago and hundreds of other styles. The earlier you start using this tool, the more useful it becomes.

- **Dictionary and Thesaurus**
  You'll find many online or via a phone app. The old-school big thick book works just fine, too. Make sure to have both a dictionary (to look up words you don't know) and a thesaurus (to find words similar to the one you're thinking of). You'll use both for reading assignments and writing papers. Use them frequently. There's no shame in not knowing and looking up a word, only in being too proud to learn something new.

- **Microsoft Office**
  No, they're not paying me to say this. I say it only because these word-processing, email, spreadsheet, and other programs are used so frequently in corporate, medical, higher education, and government sectors that being familiar with them will serve you well while taking notes or job hunting.

- **Program-specific Software**

  Depending on your area of study, there will be software that is standard in your field. For instance, social sciences use different research programs, and accounting courses use specific spreadsheets. This is why you'll want to learn about what your program recommends. You'd hate to get into an engineering program that requires you to learn computer-assisted drawing only to discover your computer can't handle the program. Also, when it comes to job hunting after graduation, being able to show your experience with this field-specific software looks great on your resume. Finally, remember that as a student you probably qualify for college software discounts. If you can afford it, I'd recommend you purchase them sometime while you're in school and still have that golden .edu email suffix that gives you educational discounts.

- **ChatGPT and AI**

  It goes without saying that we're on the verge of a text, video, audio, and visual art revolution. Amidst all of this, you will encounter dozens of opportunities to use these platforms and programs in your studies. Be aware that there is a thin line between making reasonable use of software to support your studies and using it to cheat. Regularly ask yourself, "Is this software helping me learn better or enabling me to skip the learning to just get the grade?" Which one do you think will serve you much better in the long run?

- **Backing Up Your Work**

  Of course, there are lots of ways to do this. I don't have strong feelings about how you do it. Just *do it*. Use the cloud, campus networks, thumb drives, or your grandmother's CDs. Just make sure you have systems to save your work.

## *Evaluate and Re-evaluate*

In this section we've focused on five ways to set yourself up for excellent reading and study habits. We started with your state of mind. We worked at being honest about our college insecurities and explored ways to manage our imposter phenomena. We walked through some best practices and tools for organizing your schedule and routine. We took a good look at how going to school affects those closest to you and how to make your college adventure one that your family and friends can all become part of. We imagined what a perfect reading space looks like and the specific steps you can use to support your relaxed alertness. Finally, we tuned up your tech plan. What do you have? What do you need? What can you reasonably afford?

These are some of the most important parts of succeeding at school. In wrapping up this section, there's one last thing to consider. Just as your schedule, people, space, and technology will be different from everyone else's, your plans will also change over time. Your classes, work schedule, and family's and friends' plans will change. You might find that cozy spot in the library is putting you to sleep or you need to turn your home study into a bedroom for your growing family. Maybe your computer goes out or you're getting headaches and probably should go back to the eye doctor.

At the end of each term or semester, take a few minutes to set aside your reading and look over how things are going. What parts of your setup are working, not working, or need to be tweaked? In my experience, there is rarely a perfect arrangement, but there are some plans that are better than others. Adjust what you can to create a relaxed, alert space where you can truly concentrate.

CHAPTER FOUR

# Doing the Work: Reading and Taking Notes

Having put a lot of work into setting up your reading world, you might find this section of "doing the work" a bit anticlimactic. In many ways, the setup is the hard part. Once you've examined your mindset, organized your schedule, created your spaces, talked with your people, and figured out your tech, the actual reading part becomes much easier.

It's time to dive into the techniques that will help you become a great college reader. This section walks through the best reading and note-taking strategies using seven key questions. The answers to these might seem obvious at first glance. I'd recommend you not jump to conclusions too quickly. Some of the answers are a bit counterintuitive and surprising. Use these questions to help craft your reading strategies.

## Why Am I Reading This?

Okay, that's a simple one, right? Your first answer might be, "Because it's on the syllabus," or "The professor said we had to," or "If I don't, I'll fail the midterm." All of these are acceptable answers (this is not a pop quiz), but none of them really get at what I'm asking. I'm asking, "Why am I reading this?" because before we begin reading, we need to know what it is we're looking for in these pages. Try thinking about it this way.

I suspect most of the time when we get a reading assignment, we leave class, maybe go eat lunch, and then go find our perfect spot and start reading. It may take about sixty minutes to read all the pages assigned. When we finish reading, we move on to the next thing.

Nope, wrong answer! Before you even begin reading, take a couple of minutes to think about how this connects with what you're learning in class. Answering the "Why am I reading this?" question not only speeds up your reading but will improve your grades. Here's how you do it.

First, get out your syllabus and look through your readings for the week. You'll quickly see that you might need to read a chapter or two in a textbook, a reading posted online, or part of a novel. You'll also see when these readings are due. Since we've walked through all these different types of readings already, you have a feel for how they're laid out.

Then ask yourself, "What is the professor wanting me to get out of this?" If you're taking Corporate Accounting, they may want you to understand the difference between business and personal tax processes. If you're taking Anatomy and Physiology, they may want you to memorize the structural features of the heart. If you're taking English Literature, they may want you to know the key characters and begin to identify relationships and subplots in the novel.

The point is: don't just start reading without thinking about what you're reading for. That is a formula for letting your eyes meander from paragraph to paragraph without finding anything to hold onto. Knowing why you're reading this item for a particular reason makes you focus because you are hunting for the answer to a question. You will make much better use of your time and leave with what your professor was hoping you'd learn (and that will likely appear on the next quiz).

# Should I Be Taking Notes?

Yes.

Note-taking goes hand in hand with reading. Abundant research reveals that taking notes on what you're reading significantly improves your ability to not only remember and recall information, but also do all that higher-level Bloom's Taxonomy work like comparing ideas, forming arguments, and being creative. Taking notes requires you to think about and translate what you're reading or hearing into something you put down in your words. This engagement with your reading drives learning. So, yes. Take notes.

But how!? You probably have a few habits and go-to note-taking strategies you use already. That's great if you do;

knowing what works for you is important. But if you're not sure about what works best for you, that's fine, too. In this section we'll walk through a variety of different note-taking strategies. As we've noted before (so to speak) there are few hard-and-fast rules. Experiment with these strategies and learn which ones work best for you.

## What Should I Take Notes On?

Everything. But this is a tricky question. When I say everything, I don't mean that you copy word for word from the textbook, article, or chapter you are reading. And I don't mean that more notes are necessarily better.

When I say everything, I mean you should have a few notes about every item you read. If you read a chapter, you should have notes on it. If you watch a YouTube video, you should have some notes on it. If you read an article, you should have notes on it: sometimes pages, sometimes only a few sentences. But you should have a little something on everything. The trick is to learn how to take the right kind and right amount of notes on whatever you are reading. We'll walk through exactly how to do this in just a bit.

## Handwriting or Typing? Paper or Screens?

What about handwriting vs. keyboarding? Typing has traditionally been great because it's easy to read, share, file, and search, and some folks type faster than they can write. On the flip side, it's easy to be distracted by email and social media notifications if you're working on a computer, and typing reduces retention and conceptual learning. Handwriting is preferred because it requires more focus and allows you to doodle and draw pictures, which helps your comprehension and retention. Again, the flip side is that it tends to be less organized, hard to digitally file, and most folks write slower than they can type.

There are two other important things to keep in mind here. First, there's mounting evidence that it's better to handwrite your notes than it is to type them.[35] Remember how brain science talks about spatial vs. rote memory? Positioning writing on a page, drawing pictures, etc. pushes information into this spatial memory. Second, many of the typing advantages are being transformed by improved software. Applications that translate your handwriting into typed characters and tablets that can take, file, and search notes give you the traditional advantages of typing while you are writing by hand.

Is there a difference between using paper or digital media for handwriting? I've not found evidence supporting one or the other in terms of which improves your retention and comprehension. This is probably a question of personal preference and resources (for instance, you can buy a lot of pens and spiral notebooks for the cost of a new tablet). Remember, too, that using a tablet and a note-taking program allows you to edit, share, and file your materials more easily than using lined filler paper.

My recommendations? On the one hand, listen to your preferences. If you find yourself thinking that I'm too old school to suggest paper instead of digital note-taking, no worries; use what works for you. For me? I use typing to take notes on material I'm reading. I create a new document for each item I read to annotate, or for all the materials in a particular class session. Then I open these notes on a tablet when I get to class. I take notes on my tablet and add notes to my readings at the same time. I've not touched paper for a long time.

## What's the Best Way to Take Notes on Readings in College?

You may already have some note-taking strategies. That's cool. I'd not suggest you necessarily give these up. The best way to take notes is the way that works best for you. If you've been away from note-taking for a while, this is a good time to start fresh. If you have a system you really like, this is a good time to ask if your methods are working.

I've gathered fourteen of the most common, creative, and effective note-taking strategies in the next few pages. Remember that the goal of taking notes is not to copy down everything. *The goal is to use note-taking to increase engagement with the text.* Use these strategies to genuinely connect with the reading in ways that make you wonder, tussle, ask questions, and tether your personal experiences to the content.

To help you with this, I've created a free downloadable note-taking template at gutsycollege.com. The template includes examples of all these note-taking styles. It is also formatted in Microsoft Word (.docx) so you can download it and make it your own. We'll be looking at some additional ways to use this template in later sections, too. Before you go on, this is a good time to download that template. You'll find it useful.

## The Note-taking Strategies

1. **Bullet Points and Numbering:** This is where you take ideas and make easily identifiable lists by putting a little dot in front of the sentence. This is a great way to take a longer chunk of text and distill the main ideas. Further, numbering allows you to prioritize and put things into a specific order. This can be useful if you're trying to learn a certain list of steps.

2. **Outlining:** This takes bulleting and numbering a step further by organizing groups of groups. Like creating a list, it is a valuable way to capture the main ideas. The work your brain needs to do to try and filter out all the less important information and get down to the central idea is part of that engaged reading we've been talking about.

3. **Mind Mapping:** Sounds technical, but it is simple. As you read, write key phrases or ideas in your notes. Illustrate them with colors or shapes. As you encounter more ideas, write and illustrate these and then connect them with others on your page. Jot a few notes reminding

yourself how they're connected. Think of this as a cross between doodling and note-taking that connects ideas to each other.

4. **Annotating or Paraphrasing:** This is where you take a reading and, in a sentence or two, write out a summary in your own words. Imagine this as an exercise where you force yourself to explain to your cousin the main idea of this reading in three sentences or less. You may find this process a considerable mental workout. It also will leave you with a gem of a study summary. When it's time for midterms or writing a paper, this annotation will bounce back to your mind. Annotating is one of my favorite note-taking techniques.

5. **Quotations:** I am not a fan of writing out whole sections of text in your notes *except* when you encounter a quotation that concisely captures a central idea. In this case, writing out quotations is essential. Think of them as something you might use in a paper you're writing. Quotations should be no more than a few sentences. Copy them into your notes, clearly identify them as taken from the reading, and include the page number where you found them. This will prevent you from accidentally claiming the quote as your own idea. Finally, make sure you've added this reading to your reference software. It will make citing the quotation a snap.

6. **Answering Key Questions:** Create a list of key questions that you keep at the top of every page on which you're

taking notes. The note-taking template I mentioned at gutsycollege.com has a list of recommended questions included. As you move through your reading, answer these questions in your notes. I've included some of my favorites here:

- What is the main point or argument in this reading?

- What are the key supporting points in this reading?

- What are the strengths and weaknesses of this reading?

- How does this reading respond to other things we've been reading?

- How does this reading connect with real-world situations?

- How does this reading challenge other things we're reading?

- What questions pop to mind when I read this?

- What do you agree or disagree with and why? (Always include your reasons for why—it makes your brain work!)

You don't need to answer all of these for every reading. Using them as prompts will give you a good starting point as you're taking notes.

7. **Writing Your Own Questions:** Likewise, as you move through your reading and note-taking, write out

questions that come to you. These may be more factual sorts of questions such as, "How long can second graders sit for a lesson before getting them up to move?" These may be more theoretical sorts of questions such as, "How does Octavia E. Butler's vision of fascist apocalypticism in her novel *Parable of the Sower* apply to twenty-first-century US politics?" Writing questions not only gives you things to ask during class, but also forces your brain to engage the material.

8. **Looking Up Words:** Speaking of questions, what do you do when you encounter words you don't know? First, don't be embarrassed! I felt so much better about my reading in graduate school when my PhD advisor shared that she constantly looks up words she doesn't know. Second, yes, bookmark a good dictionary or thesaurus on your phone, look up words you don't know, and write them in your notes. Maybe use a specific color in your notes for words and their definitions.

9. **Flash Cards:** Speaking of words, should you use flash cards? These can be great tools. I had some students who lived by their flash card decks. They are particularly useful for words and their definitions or working at memorizing lists of concepts, bones in the body, species of animals, etc. There are some clever software programs that let you create flash cards and practice them online. Although I don't have studies to support it, I suspect that handwritten flash cards are more effective than online tools because you're forced to write them out and your

brain spatially connects images on paper to ideas in your head. I can still remember some words because of the coffee stain or bent corner on a flash card.

10. **Drawing:** I do it all the time in my notes. Consider using shapes, doodles, colors, and other visuals in your notes to illustrate and connect ideas. Think of this as a less organized version of the mind-mapping strategy we looked at earlier. This can work well for those with a creative edge that needs to be set free while taking notes. Use shapes, images, lines, arrows, faces, land-scapes, overlapping diagrams, tables, and every other imaginable doodle that comes to mind to show relation-ships. Combining drawing with written notes can work well. If I could take all my notes by doodling, I would.

11. **Highlighters:** Some folks love highlighters; some hate them. I confess I'm not quite a hater, but close to it. Like every other note-taking strategy we've looked at, the question is, do highlighters increase your genuine engagement with the reading? In my experience, students highlight too much (especially in textbooks). If you like highlighters, use them sparingly and only to iden-tify important ideas. Don't fool yourself into thinking that just because you have a page dripping with neon yellow ink, you've learned something. Find ways to engage!

12. **Writing In Your Books:** Compared to highlighters, this is a much more engaging way to interact with your books. If you are planning on keeping your paperback, underline

important concepts, circle key words, mark the begin-ning of new sections, scribble notes, and jot questions in the margins. If you have a digital copy, try taking notes on a tablet with a smart pen. Writing is much more engaging than splattering neon paint all over the page. When you're ready to take some notes on the reading, you'll have already recorded your ideas in the margins.

13. **Other Note-taking Ideas**: I'm constantly amazed with my students' creativity. Don't be afraid to try new strategies or technology. Some I've come to appreciate recently: organizing a few friends to create a shared cloud document to pool notes, or using specific colors in their notes to represent certain things (e.g., one color for definitions of words, one color for main ideas, one color for questions they have). My personal favorite was a student who kept notes mentally stimulating by writing in the Dwarvish language in one class, Elvish in another class, and Klingon in another class. Impressive!

14. **A Note about Friends and Notes**: Dividing up readings with friends or creating a shared document can be useful. Just be careful here. Don't let teamwork under-mine your engagement. For example, say five of you each agree to do a short write-up on two chapters of a ten-chapter book and then share them with each other. Good job, very efficient! But that also means you've not really had to think about eight chapters. If you do this, make sure to also do your own brief summary of each chapter that you could then add your friends' notes

to. Otherwise, your clever efficiency will lose you 80 percent of the book's meaning.

Want to know the absolute very best way to take notes in class? Experiment and create your own method where you don't just breeze through a bunch of words on the page or copy everything down. What is the key to great reading and note-taking? Yes, that's right—engagement! Excellent note-taking is about actively using your curiosity and really chewing on what you're reading. That's how you remember more, recall more, and learn more. It's what will both increase your efficiency and drive your grades up.

# How Do I Read and Take Notes on Different Sorts of Readings?

We've walked through lots of different ways to effectively take notes on your readings. You might be wondering where to begin or if some strategies work better than others. Great question! If you want to take your note-taking skills to the next level, it's worth thinking about how you use these strategies as you approach different sorts of readings.

As you well know, there are different genres of writing: fiction books, magazine articles, classroom textbooks, academic articles, blogs, tweets, and so on. All are writing, but they are very different types of writing. And of course, you already know that you don't read a tweet in the same way you read a handwritten letter from your grandmother in the same way you read a chemistry textbook. The challenge is to learn how to read and take notes on different things in different ways.

The hints below combine Chapter 2's description of the different types of readings you encounter in college with the reading and note-taking hints we just walked through. Again, remember that your goal here is to find a system that helps you genuinely engage with the reading. I'll share some of my favorite strategies, but make sure to tweak these for yourself.

## Textbooks

Textbooks, the big thick books that often have glossy pages and color pictures, have a reading level on the easier side. Remember that the ideas are usually clearly structured, presented in an outline format, and tend to be heavy on foundational concepts and terms.

How do you read and take notes here? Remember the learning models we discussed at the beginning of the book (Bloom, Bain, etc.)? Textbooks are often used at the first floor of Bloom's pyramid. Your goal here is to master the basic terminology and perspectives of whatever field you're in— business, welding, social work, chemistry, etc.—so you can build on them in later classes.

Two temptations to avoid. First, don't unleash gallons of highlighter on those poor glossy pages. You may well find yourself with page after page dripping with neon ink. Second, don't just read the all-too-convenient outlined summary at the end of the chapter and think you're good to go.

**The Strategy**

- Give the chapter a solid skimming to see how it's structured. Is it a long chronological timeline? Is it built around
five prominent people or ideas? Does it walk you through
six specific techniques? A quick overview will give you a
sense of what sort of reading and note-taking techniques
will be most useful.

- Go back to the beginning of the chapter. As you work
through the sections, create flash cards for every term
and idea you don't know. Review the pile for ten to fifteen
minutes once a day. I like to start with about fifty cards,
and when I identify one correctly, I set it aside. When I miss
one, I shuffle it back into the pile. I keep eliminating them
until I'm able to identify them all. Repetition is important
here. Keep adding cards and repeating daily until the terms
are familiar. By the way, you will learn much more with ten
minutes a day for six days than with a single thirty-minute
day of cramming (and it's way less painful).

- Create a mind map in your notes. This works well with
textbooks because the outline format tends to start with
a large central idea and then moves into subcategories.
Drawing these out on a page with symbols, images, and
colors will begin to create spatial connections in your
brain. You'll likely find that you begin to remember things
not just as a term with a plain definition, but because it
appears on the upper-right side of your page in the shape
of a tree with green leaves shaped in certain ways. Or as a

bike wheel with a central hub and spokes of various ideas radiating out from it.

- Use the questions that appear at the end of sections or the chapter and write out the answers in your own words. These questions usually capture the essence of the chapter's main points. Don't just silently come up with answers in your head. Actually write them out in your notes. Answering these will not only force you to hunt for the correct information, but the action of formulating an answer in your own words and writing it into a document will create that mental engagement your brain needs for retention and recall. These written answers will also be golden for your exam review!

## Edited Books

Made up of shorter readings often written by important scholars in a particular field, there may be ten to twelve or more readings in an edited book. They provide perspectives on the topic from a bunch of different directions. The reading level is likely more difficult than the textbook.

How do you read and take notes here? Back to the learning models we looked at in the beginning of the book. Edited books are almost certainly connected to something you learned about in your introductory classes, but they are going into more detail. Professors often assign these in 200- or 300-level classes for just these reasons. Edited books are building the next floors up in Bloom's blueprints.

One temptation to avoid: you might think starting at the beginning and running through to the end is the best approach, sort of like reading a novel. You're likely to get frustrated and waste quite a bit of time doing this because you don't have a good sense of what this text is about.

**The Strategy**

- Always start by slowly and purposefully reading *only* the introduction and preface (if there is one). These sorts of works typically begin with an overview of the whole book, how it's set up, what the sections are, and why different works are included here. It sometimes includes a brief summary of each work. Read this repeatedly until you have a good sense of the overall book.

- Remember that each chapter or section is a distinctive work. Each of these chapters has its own thesis, purpose, evidence, etc.

- As you tackle each chapter, read the introduction and conclusion of each, and give the whole chapter a brief skim to see how it's set up. Is it laid out like an outline? Are there four main sections (that you can tackle one at a time)? How is the author setting up this reading to make a point?

- Once again, make flash cards for unfamiliar terminology. If you don't know it, look it up, write it down, and review it daily until you know it.

- Watch for signposts. These are markers in the reading that give you organizing hints. For example, an author may write, "There are four reasons this would be the case. First …" Or they might write, "We'll begin thinking about environmental policies at the local level, then move through the state, national, and international perspectives." These signposts help you see where the writer is headed. Use them to understand your reading and structure your note-taking. Jotting a little note in the margin or circling the first word in a paragraph when you find a signpost can also be a helpful habit.

- Mind mapping by writing out main ideas and drawing pictures and lines showing how they are connected can be useful here, too. You can do this for both individual chapters and for the book as a whole. It's a great way to track how all the sections relate to each other.

- If you're planning on keeping the book, underline key ideas as you read and then scribble notes and questions in the margins.

- This is also an opportunity to use those questions we were talking about. Keep a set of questions on a note-taking template page and answer them. If you've not downloaded this free template, go grab it at gutsycollege.com.

- The strategy I use most often is a combination of annotation and outlining. I start with a three-sentence summary of the chapter followed by a brief outline of the main ideas. Always use your own words because you're forcing your brain to work! How deeply you go into this outline is up to you. I try to get my annotation and outline onto half a page. Too short and you can't get at the main ideas; too long and it feels like you're starting to rewrite the whole chapter. Again, this becomes a fantastic tool for not just reading, but also exam prep and finding material to include in papers you're writing.

## Research Articles

As mentioned before, research articles are usually shorter (maybe twenty to forty pages) and likely explore a specific topic with great depth. When I say specific, I do mean specific. These are generally written by professors, researchers, or other experts in a particular field and explore a partic-ular research question by gathering data, analyzing it, and reporting its findings. The reading level is usually quite chal-lenging. They tend to be used more as you move from 200- to 300- to 400-level classes.

Note that a research article tends to use a particular writing structure. In general, it follows what is known as the scientific method. It has an introduction, followed by a literature review walking through the other research already out there about this topic. Then it will show how the question or research is different from or expands on others. Most articles will show you how they collected data, how they analyzed it, what they discovered, and how this answers the research question they're asking.

As with edited books, it is tempting to just jump in and begin reading. And as with edited books, you're likely to get frustrated and waste quite a bit of time doing this because you don't have a good sense of what this article is about.

**The Strategy**

Your strategy here will be very similar to chapters in edited books, with a couple of tweaks:

- First, ask yourself why the professor assigned this. Sometimes they want you to understand the conclusions of the article. Sometimes they want you to see how the research was conducted. Sometimes there are concepts they're trying to introduce you to. Instead of spending hours trying to understand every little detail, ask yourself what the professor is wanting you to glean from it and focus on those purposes.

- From here, use the same strategies outlined in the edited books section above:

  - In general, you'll probably start by slowly and purposefully reading *only* the introductory and concluding sections.

  - Give the whole article a brief skim to see how it's set up.

  - Flash cards and terminology: if you don't know it, look it up, write it down, and review it daily until you do.Mind map by writing out main ideas and drawing pictures and lines showing how they are connected.

- Underline key ideas as you read and then scribble notes and questions in the margins. Don't forget to impress your professor with your fantastic questions!

- Use prompting questions to think through and write out answers (see gutsycollege.com for these questions).

- And still my favorite: in your own words, write a three-sentence summary of the chapter followed by a brief outline of the main ideas.

- When working with academic research articles, you'll probably find an outline built into the reading for you. A useful way to take notes here is to write responses to the questions built into the scientific method. Write a summary of the purpose of the article, then a couple of sentences summarizing:

  - The literature review: Make a brief descriptive list of the previous research or ideas this research article is rooted in.

  - The data and research method: Briefly summarize the methods used to conduct this research. Did the authors use surveys, interviews, chemical analysis of water samples, counts of certain bugs in a one-square-foot area of rainforest, data downloaded from other sources, or maybe a combination?

  - The way the data was analyzed: A couple-sentence description of how the data they collected was analyzed. Did they use statistical analysis, coding of statements made by interview respondents, or other approaches?

- ○ The key conclusions: A short summary of what the authors have discovered because of this research. Keep it brief and include the main conclusions.

You should end up with a set of notes that have condensed the whole reading to less than a page. This becomes a great tool for remembering what you've read, studying for exams, and writing papers!

## *Monographs*

I think of this as what we used to call "a book." Think of it as a nonfiction version of a novel. This is a piece of work, usually by a single author, who is writing something that lays out a well-developed vision for their perspective or argument. They're often several hundred pages long, and the reading difficulty can range from accessible to challenging. They tend to have a specific focus (sort of like research articles) but are taking more time to flesh out their perspective. Because they're longer and are building on the basics you learned in your 100-level classes, professors tend to start using them in your 200 classes and beyond.

There are several things that are good to know about monographs. First, unlike textbooks, they're going to assume you know the basics of the field. Also, unlike research articles, they rarely follow a specific formula. Because they can be written in all sorts of ways, it's important to get a good feel for how the author is setting it up. Authors often do you a huge favor by taking some time in the introduction to explain what they're doing. You'll likely find a few pages in the introduction where they write, "In Chapter 1 I explain …" then "In Chapter 2 we'll explore why …" and "In Chapter 3 we'll turn our attention to …" Search for this and use it as a map for your reading.

**The Strategy**

How do you tackle reading and taking notes on monographs? Tweak, but still use many of the same strategies outlined above:

- Flash cards and terminology: If you don't know it, look it up, write it down, and review it daily until you do.Mind mapping might still be helpful, but because you're reading something more focused, you may not be encountering as many ideas that need connecting.

- Underlining key ideas as you read and then scribbling notes and questions in the margins is useful here. This will help you think about the author's arguments and ideas.

- Use prompting questions to think through and write out answers as you move through chapter by chapter (see gutsycollege.com for these questions).

- Write out particularly poignant quotations in your notes. Remind yourself that they are not your words, and include the page number for where you found each one.

When working with monographs, a useful way to take notes here is to work chapter by chapter. Write a three-sentence paraphrase of the chapter and add several bullet points, a short outline of the key ideas, or several questions for each chapter. Aim for no more than half a page per chapter. I like to keep this in a single document that, once again, is a great tool for exam preparation or paper writing.

## How-to Texts

Depending on your program, you might also be reading about how to do things that are specific to your field. Nursing students will be reading about how to properly start an IV, diesel mechanics will read about how to change out glow plugs, and computer technicians will read about how to defend against the most common phishing strategies. Professors will assign particular texts so you can read about how to properly do something and learn to avoid some of the frequent mistakes folks can make.

The difficulty of these texts can be highly selective, as in, if you know the field, you might find it easy; if you don't, you might feel like you're reading a foreign language. For instance, I might be able to read doctoral-level social science but would be totally lost reading engine repair 101 (thank goodness for mechanics!). Finally, these readings are often designed with action in mind. They describe the right way to do something with the expectation that a nursing student will practice hundreds of needle sticks under the eye of someone who has started thousands of them.

How to take notes here? Because of their design, this is a hard question to answer. If you get a notebook full of photocopied pages, it could be that writing notes on the pages works best. If the text is entirely online, you'll need to find ways to digitally scribble in the margins or create your own pages of notes using the strategies we've already outlined.

In addition to thinking carefully about how to take notes so you can understand what you're reading, you might also think about how you could use this text in the future. For instance, is this something you might want to laminate and keep in your pocket while on the floor in the hospital? Is it a notebook you'll keep on the shelf in the shop so you can quickly find the different number of threads on fine, metric, or standard metal screws? How can you organize yourself now to make things easier later?

## Miscellaneous Readings

Besides textbooks, edited books, research articles, monographs, and how-to texts, you'll encounter all sorts of other readings. Classes I've taught have included blogs, novels, student newspaper editorials, magazine articles, and letters. You'll be looking at all sorts of online charts, postings, and research. And although they're not really readings, you'll probably encounter recordings of speeches, YouTube videos, and full-length movies.

So, how do you take notes on these? As you might guess, it varies a lot depending on the item you're looking at and what it is the professor wants you to get out of it.

### The Strategy

- Remember that learning, remembering, and recalling ideas happens when you engage with the material. You need to interact with this editorial, speech, or handbook.

- If there is space to underline key ideas as you're reading, do it.

- If you can write notes or questions in the margins or underline key points, do it.

- Write a few notes about everything. Again, I recommend a three-sentence paraphrase in your own words and at least three bullet points that include the central ideas. This works well for miscellaneous materials ranging from films and audio recordings to speeches and online charts.

## Overview

Again, what you are aiming for with your note-taking here is:

1. a piece of work in your own words
2. that captures the main idea and a few key points
3. for *every item you read*.

Even a little bit is better than nothing. You'll find that sometimes it takes only a few words to bring your mind back to that video you were watching in class. Having a few thoughts written about something will cue your mind and take you back to what it was you were reading or watching.

And don't forget to make good use of your reference software.

As you take notes on these materials, pause a moment to enter the citation information into your reference software every time you start a new reading. These thirty seconds will save you hours later. Make it a simple habit. You'll thank yourself!

Does this seem like a lot? If you've never taken notes like this before, it might be something to get used to. However, as you do it more, it becomes second nature. And, because you're better able to remember and track the ideas through the notes you've taken, writing papers, posting online comments, and completing other projects becomes much faster since you're not looking high and low to find that one quote you sort of remember but don't recall which page or reading it came from. After doing this consistently for a month or two, you'll find it becomes an efficient habit.

## How Do I Keep Track of All This Stuff!?

Taking even a single college class generates lots of notes, papers, and thoughts. Although folks don't usually talk about it, having a filing system for your reading notes is essential. It's worth taking a bit of time to think about how you are going to do this before settling on your note-taking system.

I'll date myself and share that tablets, laptops, and cloud storage were not a thing when I was in college. Everyone took notes using spiral-bound notebooks or loose-leaf lined pages of paper that we'd snap into three-ring binders. My filing system back then? Usually a notebook for every class.

Some folks still prefer this old-school approach. But things get a bit more complicated when you're downloading readings or accessing them online. You might take lecture notes on paper in class but use your laptop to take reading notes. You might use a tablet to take notes in class but then have a set of folders on your laptop to keep other things in. Or maybe you're using a cloud platform to do most everything, except for the scribbles in the margins of the books you buy. The issue here isn't that there's one right way to do it, but that the variety of options means you have both a larger quantity and a more diverse set of materials to keep track of.

## *Create Categories*

At a minimum, I'd recommend you think of your classes as categories. For example, I like to store notes, readings, and other materials in a folder on my computer with a number, date, and name: "SOC 152 (F19) Introduction to Sociology" (in this case, F means Fall). Each document I create will reflect this category; for example, all my reading notes might be titled, "SOC 152 (F19) Week 1 Reading Notes (history of sociology)." I add a two- or three-word description in parentheses to remind me what we were talking about in Week 1. I might keep my class notes as a single running file named "SOC 152 (F19) Class Notes." Papers you write can carry a similar tag.

You can use different media and storage, but choose a common class name for everything. When you finish a class, put everything in that single folder and archive it. You'll likely return to older materials, so file things in a way that you'll remember. Keep it simple. Once you get it set up, stick with it. At the end of the semester or term, go back and file everything. At the beginning of a new one, set things up for the next set of classes. Don't feel obligated to use my system, but do find a routine that allows you to easily keep track of your current work and know how to find it in the future.

## Back Up!

It probably goes without saying that you should back up your work in cloud storage, campus networks, or your own external hard drive. You'll probably ignore this suggestion until you lose something valuable. Once you've lost a paper, you'll come to appreciate how important it is to back up your work. If you learn to do this before you've lost something you've worked hard on, you're a wiser person than I.

# CHAPTER FIVE

# *Final Notes on Reading in College*

**W**e've walked through what reading is about and reviewed a long list of strategies for how to do a great job reading and taking notes in college. Although it is tempting to stop here, I want to share a few final thoughts. Some of these suggestions come from my own experience with hundreds of students. Some of these grow from reading reflections on other parts of my life, studies, and work.

These six ideas also grow from my sense that there's more to be gleaned from reading than most people realize. These perspectives are less about giving you specific suggestions for how to read and more about standing back and asking some bigger questions about reading.

Although these reflections may not seem directly related to your college reading work, you might be surprised. Recognizing some of these reading perspectives will likely lead to better grades. Working these into your class questions or incorporating them into a paper you're writing will impress your professor. Some of these might give you some insight into yourself.

Read on and see what you think.

# Indulgent Reading

I love to read, but I feel guilty about it almost every day.

While writing this book about helping college students read better in school, I encountered an odd feeling. Sort of like when you're driving and begin hearing a tiny, almost inaudible clicking in the car that you're pretty sure wasn't there yesterday. The sort of sound that makes you stop, listen, and wonder if it's real or if you're just hearing things.

This strange reading guilt clicking in my mind doesn't make sense to me. If I genuinely enjoy reading, why do I feel this little twinge of guilt when I sit down to read? I suspect that not everyone feels this way. I'm guessing some of you might be reading this and wondering, "Huh? I don't get it. I've never felt that." Good on you. But for the others who feel a similar pinch of guilt when picking up a book, join me in wondering about this together.

I was relieved to learn that I'm not the only one who feels this way.[36] For some, reading fiction in particular can feel trivial or indulgent. Since most of us can't directly connect it to our daily work routine (even if one's work is reading or writing!) it can still feel like we're wasting time and being unproductive.

## *Why!?*

Where did this come from? As a social scientist, I'm convinced that the community we're raised in has a powerful effect on us. My mom was a kindergarten teacher, and I often remember her reading the local newspaper in the evening. My dad still reads many Westerns today. Although I don't remember there being lots of books around the house, a set of *World Book* encyclopedias is permanently imprinted in my memory. I remember the salesman at the house selling them to us. I remember that they were the 1976 bicentennial edition, which had red, white, and blue covers. And I remember how they all sat in alphabetical order in a glossy, dark-stained, two-story wooden rack in the northeast corner of the living room, which had green shag carpet and a brick fireplace (remember that spatial memory we talked about!?). In short, yes, there were books around our home.

At the same time, I got the impression from my community that reading wasn't that important. Building stuff, hard manual labor, athletic prowess, and "dirt under your nails" was where it was at. To be valued was to be able to show what you've built or the long hours you've worked. I'm not saying these things aren't important. Just that for those of us who loved reading, it took some effort to find our place. In hindsight, I think I found "my people" in the high school debate team and during research trips to the local university libraries.

In addition to the childhood ponds we swim in, we're also marinated in messages about what matters. Our cultural heroes are athletic and musical celebrities, headline-catching politicians, and billionaire CEOs. Teachers, librarians, authors, and journalists fade into the background. Rewards go to those who appear on screens and who have money. It's not quite this simple, of course. Many of our athletes, musicians, politicians, and CEOs are well-read. It's just that reading is not celebrated as a virtue in the same way physical strength, political power, musical fame, or sheer wealth is glamorized in much of the world.

Because of this, some can find the joy of reading indulgent. Reading can feel like a waste of time when measured against messages we received growing up or through our constant consumption of social media. This feeling can also come from the daily demands of keeping the rest of our lives, family, household, etc., together. How dare we take time to read when there's laundry, car repair, mowing, fixing dinner, getting the kids to practice, and a hundred other things to do!?

## *Think Differently*

So how do we begin to think differently about reading as a part of our lives? A few reflections have been helpful for me …

- Remember that reading is good for you.[37] Among other things, it improves your vocabulary, knowledge base, memory, and ability to speak more clearly. Reading is as much of an investment in your health as getting good sleep and regular exercise.

- Reading fiction in particular strengthens our ability to think creatively, helps us relate to others more empathetically, and draws us into the contextual complexity of life.[38] Reading fiction allows us to grow as human beings. Interesting people read.

- Read within your means.[39] Although Nicola Alter, the author of this blog posting, is reflecting on Reading Guilt as a feeling of not reading enough, I think the suggestion addresses our struggle as well. If you feel guilty about reading when you perceive there are other "more important" things to do, block out a set time as reading time. This is the time you commit to caring for your reading well-being. To invest in your reading doesn't mean abandoning all your other responsibilities. You are carving out time for reading amidst everything else that is also important.

- Remember that reading and your education are not just about you. They can also be about moving your people forward. Your success, health, and education ripple through the lives of everyone around you. In fact, when you can enter school as the member of a team, where those around you are making changes so you can take classes, your studying becomes their success, too. (This is why that early section of the book about setting up your people is so important)!

- As you enter school, remember that reading is your work now, or at least part of your work. I've found it helpful to understand studying as part of my job. I've signed up for this class or program. I'm paying money for it. I'm doing it to accomplish a goal my family and I have agreed is important. To read is to get out of bed, get dressed, brush my teeth, and show up for work.

- For many, reading is an (almost) totally free getaway. Although introverts might need this more than extroverts, most folks could regularly use some time away from the stresses of work, relationships, finances, and life's daily stresses. Reading can take you away, even if for just a bit.

- Join a group of readers. One of the best ways to push back against messages saying that reading doesn't matter is to hang out with others who know that it does. Find your people and read together.

- And last but not least, you deserve to have this time. With everything else you're doing to tend to the needs of folks around you, make it a priority to be a bit indulgent and take time to explore history or psychology or a great story. You deserve to take time to read and grow.

Moving beyond the messages we've received about reading that leave us feeling like it doesn't matter that much is no easy task. Be gracious with yourself, take small steps, and keep at it. Reading can be one of the most powerful tools for relieving your stress, strengthening your health, and improving your creativity and career. Read on!

# Critical Reading

Have you ever been on a date or in a friendship that just doesn't seem to be working? One of the reasons friendships or relationships don't work is because someone is afraid to go deeper, to really ask questions, share with each other, listen, and learn about each other in deeper ways.[40] Shallow conversations might work for a while, but without that deeper knowledge, things will probably get boring pretty fast.

You might be wondering what any of this has to do with "critical reading." Well, stay with me here a bit ...

The first time I heard the words "critical reading" was in my first college class. It was a religious studies course where we were reading a variety of texts from different religious traditions. We were told we were going to be "reading critically," and I confess that I didn't really know what that meant.

Or, rather, I should say that I thought it meant we were supposed to be looking for problems with the reading, be suspicious of the author, be hunting for mistakes in the book, or be searching for a reason to not like what we're reading. I later learned that all of these are wrong and, in fact, opposite of what critical reading is about.

Critical reading (like any meaningful relationship) is about deeply and personally connecting with a reading. Shallow reading, like shallow relationships, may get you by for a while (avoiding the F, as Bain explained to us), but if you want something richer and more meaningful (whether it be a book or a friend) pushing deeper, asking questions, and listening carefully is essential. That's what critical reading is about. Sure, you'll find things you don't understand or will disagree with. Welcome to real relationships and real reading. But the point is to authentically engage, to care enough to ask real questions.

## Being Critical

So, what is critical reading? In academic parlance critical reading is,

> "the close, careful reading of a text that is undertaken in order to understand it fully and assess its merits. It is not simply a matter of skimming a text or reading for plot points; rather, critical reading requires that you read attentively and thoughtfully, taking into account the text's structure, purpose, and audience, among other characteristics (e.g., tone, mood, diction, etc.)."[41]

To put it another way, critical reading is about asking good questions and listening intently as we read a book, article, or anything else. Texts, like people, almost always have deeper things going on. We're committing to a real relationship with what we're reading.

Why do we do it? Critical reading is the only way we learn anything. Asking questions of what we're reading, why the author chose the characters, or what evidence is being used to make someone's point is how we discover what's really going on. In the same way we learn that a friend hates going in the water only after listening carefully to their story of how one of their childhood friends drowned, we only learn what a book is really about if we genuinely wonder why it's written the way it is.

## How to Be More Critical

How do we do it? There are two important steps. First, we need to think about the right sorts of questions to ask when we're reading. Second, we need some tools to do this work and keep track of what we're discovering. Let's start with the questions.

Something you'll discover in college is that there are dozens of ways to ask critical-reading questions.[42] For our purposes, I'm going to suggest seven foundational questions you can use for almost any reading:

1.  What is the main argument or "story" of this reading?

2.  Why is the writer writing this? What are they *really* trying to say?

3.  What evidence or logic is used in this writing?

4.  What do I see as the strengths and weaknesses of this reading?

5.  How does this reading respond to or interact with other readings on this topic?

6.  What are the implications of this reading? How might it apply to real-world situations?

7.  How does this reading support or challenge what I have learned from other sources?

Getting into the habit of caring about what you're reading and asking these sorts of critical questions is the first step toward understanding your reading in deeper ways.

The second step is to develop a way to keep track of the insights you uncover as you read. There are a variety of ways to do this. Experiment your way through this list and see what works for you:

- **Write in the book:** Jot notes in the margins. Scribble questions. Circle words and passages that catch your attention or seem to be central ideas.

- **Mark pages in the book:** Place mini sticky notes, or fold down or ink up the corners of the book's pages so you can find your way back to important points you discovered.

- **Chapter notes:** When you read the end of a chapter, use the blank space that often appears there to write your questions, impressions, discoveries, strengths, weaknesses, etc. These very rough thoughts will be invaluable for your work later.

- **Annotate:** Use the critical questions to write up a brief summary of what you read. Although you can do this in the blank space at the end of a book or in a handwritten journal, my personal favorite is to create a document on my computer.

- **Compare notes:** After you've gathered a few of your ideas, share them with your friends, and see if they had similar or different ideas.

- **Organize:** Keeping these notes organized in a way that you can find them is crucial. This critical-reading work becomes the starting point for writing papers, completing online postings, and preparing for exams. Make sure to create a system for filing and being able to review this work.

- **Take notes on your notes:** If you can get into a good routine where your notes are ready before class, you can add your class notes to the notes you've already taken, maybe in a different color. You'll find that this will amplify your learning because you're connecting your personal work with what's happening in class.

One of my favorite ways to track my questions and thoughts is to create a document that gathers all this together. If you hop over to gutsycollege.com you will find a free downloadable template you can use and adapt for your own work. There are many critical questions listed there that will spark your thinking.

In this section we've walked through some foundational critical questions to ask and some ways to keep track of your discoveries. But most of all, I hope we've dispelled the sense that reading critically has anything to do with trying to disparage the author, belittle the text, or disrespect the community from which a book has grown. Quite the contrary. At its best critical reading is an expression of genuine commitment to engage and listen.

# Catalyzed Reading

Let's talk catalysts. Catalysts are those things you add to a chemical reaction to speed it up.[43] In other words, you can have all the stuff you think you need to make something happen, but without a catalyst you might wait forever to get the action going.

I think reading can be this way. Sometimes, when we get an assignment, we're not really interested in it, but we know we need to read it because it'll be on the test, sooooo ... we read it. Maybe we do it sort of half-heartedly. Maybe we take a few notes. Then we move on to the next assignment or pack the kids' lunches or go binge-watch a streaming series.

We're reading, but there's no heat. No "ah-ha." No "Hey, this makes me think of that time when ..." We need something more to catalyze the learning that comes when reading mixes with our experience.

## Light My Fire

Great, so how do we do that? An idea that begins to light this fire for me was coined by Alexander Kapp and popularized by Malcolm Knowles.[44] We dug into this idea earlier when we looked at the distinction between andragogy and pedagogy and how reading and learning is different for children compared to adults:

- *peda*, which means "children" + *agogos*, which means "to lead" = pedagogy

- *andra*, which means "adult" + *agogos*, which means "to lead" = andragogy

You might be thinking the same thing I am ... "Duh! No big surprise that you teach children differently than you teach adults." But when Knowles really began looking into it, he discovered how little time we spend thinking about the differences between what children and adults bring to school, and how many of our colleges are still designed with children in mind.

You might also be asking (as a good adult learner!), "Why does any of this matter?" It matters because if we want to become excellent readers in college, we can use these andragogical realities to strengthen our reading. Each of these catalysts can spark and accelerate our learning. Rather than just reading to gather general information or collect facts that we'll work into a paper or hope to retain long enough to pass a midterm, we'll read with personal curiosity, life experience, and deeper questions in mind.

Catalyzed reading is looking for that spark that sets off the reaction between this reading and our lives. These sparks can come from many different places. In my work with students of all ages, they often come from powerful personal experiences. For example,

- I worked with a student who was returning to school because he was eager to support his family. His parents' generation immigrated to the US, struggled to learn English late in life, and worked long hours to support their kids through school. This student was eager to learn because he saw their success as an opportunity to honor his ancestors and pass this legacy on to the next generation.

- Another student was the single parent of a child who was experiencing severe learning disabilities. She was working full time and squeezing in a class here and there while grandparents provided childcare. This student recently graduated with a degree in psychology and was the leader of a local advocacy group for children on the autism spectrum. Her commitment to the families of intellectually challenged kids made its way into every project and paper. This student's fire was inspiring.

- And I've worked with hundreds of students who have recently returned from cross-cultural experiences. Their travels led them to look at their school, assignments, and reading through a new lens. It was fascinating to see how these students studying criminal justice, nutrition, or medicine looked at their classwork through not just their own eyes, but also through the eyes of those they had met in other places around the world.

I don't think we need to have a single, ultra-powerful, life-shaping experience to catalyze our learning. At its core, catalyzed reading is the rather simple commitment to find ways to bring what matters to us into our reading.

## *How to Enter the Conversation with Yourself*

How do we do this? We can use Knowles's six principles. I've listed them here with some questions. Ask these questions of whatever you happen to be reading, and follow the answers deeper into the text. If you can find ways to turn your reading into a personal conversation with something in your life or experience, you will likely find yourself more engaged in what you're reading. If you're using the note-taking template found at gutsycollege.com, you could add some of these questions to the sidebar as a convenient way to catalyze your reading.

1. Adults are self-directed learners; their curiosity is pulled forward by personal interests.

   - How does this reading connect with something that is important to me?

2. Adults accumulate experience; their learning benefits from a growing pool of life experience that they bring to their learning.

   - Where does this reading show you a new way to think about something you've experienced in your life?

3. Learning is related to social roles; adults' interests are shaped by a multitude of social roles such as being parents, spouses, community participants, neighbors, employees, supervisors, etc.

   - Does this reading reveal something new about how you relate to your family, friends, or colleagues at work?

4. Adults want to apply their knowledge; they are eager to apply their learnings to solving current problems.

   • Does this reading give you some ways to think about challenges you are experiencing in your life or profession right now?

5. Adults are more internally motivated; their learning is fueled by personal goals or commitments.

   • What are some specific ways this reading helps you move toward the goals you have set for yourself?

6. Adults need to know why; they want to know how the material matters to them.

   • Why does this reading matter to your learning? Why does this matter as part of the course? How does this reading apply to the real world?

As you think about these questions, I challenge you to resist what we might call "reading cynicism." It's that automatic reaction many students have to being assigned a reading that is unfamiliar. It's similar to the "Where will I ever use the Pythagorean theorem in real life?" question that math professors tangle with. It can be easy to quickly disregard some readings as irrelevant because they don't seem to immediately connect with our personal experience.

As a lifelong student and former professor, I find this to be a lazy reaction. And you're paying too much money to be lazy. I agree that some readings catalyze more quickly than others.

But I've rarely encountered a reading that is impossible to connect with. In fact, it is sometimes the hardest readings that have the most to offer, *if* you're willing to genuinely invest. Asking these catalyzing questions will help you do just that.

# Reflexive Reading

When we talk about reflexive reading, we're not talking about reflexes like how your leg jumps when you tap your knee in just the right spot. Reflexivity is about turning our attention back on ourselves. It's about working to recognize the assumptions and power we tend to overlook as we're doing our reading in college. That might sound a little cryptic, so here's an example.

Some years ago, I participated in a community organizing internship in Southeast Chicago. This neighborhood was very different from the small rural Oregon community I grew up in. Folks lived, talked, dressed, walked, and ate differently than where I grew up. It turns out I didn't need to travel to a different country to find what felt like a whole different world.

The differentness of this place became very real when I went shopping for the first time. I went to the little grocery store around the corner from my apartment. I was hunting for all the staples a twenty-three-year-old white college-age guy could want—frozen pizza, mac and cheese, Pop-Tarts, raisin bran—you know, the basics.

After wandering through the rows and rows of Spanish-labeled packages, I went to the counter and asked where I'd find the things on my list. Being fluently bilingual in Spanish and English, the fellow at the register pointed me to the end of aisle 10. Amazed, there in the back corner of the store I found everything I was looking for … all perfectly organized under a sign hanging from the ceiling that read "Ethnic Foods."

It took a few moments for that to sink in. Was this a joke? Me? Ethnic? I wasn't "ethnic." Where I grew up, folks who *didn't* speak English, *didn't* eat Pop-Tarts, or dressed differently than me were ethnic. Ethnic means different, foreign, unfamiliar. That's not me, is it?

Of course it was. What is "different" is always relative to what a community establishes as "normal." It may be easy to grasp this idea, but experiencing it in a grocery store I'd never been in, trying to buy things with labels I couldn't read, and finding what I was looking for in the "Ethnic Foods" section had a whole different feeling. *My* staples were not everyone's staples. I was different here. It was a jarring moment that continued throughout my internship and pushed me into a reflexive journey.

For me to begin to understand this community and build some relationships, I needed to look inside, think, and be honest about the assumptions and stereotypes I was bringing to my time in Chicago.

## Understanding Positionality

A term closely associated with reflexivity is positionality. Positionality helps us recognize that who we are influences the way we see things. Positionality explains why we interpret things differently depending on how we've been shaped by where we come from.

Back to Chicago. I was a twenty-three-year-old, middle-class white guy who spoke only English and was there as part of his graduate school program. I had moved into a primarily Mexican, lower-middle-class, mostly bilingual Spanish-/English-speaking community. My new neighbors had seen plenty of young white kids drop in to "help out these poor folks" for a week or two. These kids would come, work a bit, feel good about their generosity, and then never be heard from again. It was going to take some hard work to break down these barriers.

Some community members looked at me as just another white do-gooder college student who was here one day and gone the next. My lack of Spanish skills often left me feeling outside of the conversation and a little paranoid that folks were talking about me. One year was hardly enough time to work through these fears and hesitations. But it was enough time to discover that it was vital to ask myself harder questions about how I show up among those whose normal is not my normal.

When it comes to reading, positionality is about standing back from the words, paragraphs, and stories being told and wondering how the writing is being shaped by the perspective of the author or the image of the world that the author holds in mind.

Learning to be reflexive takes some time and requires as much un-learning as learning. It means realizing that the way each of us was raised has a powerful effect on how we see the world. Sometimes this ethnocentric default tempts us to see the world we were raised in and all the food, clothes, and other cultural values as being superior to the ways others were raised. At the very least, it can lead us to overlook important things going on around us or prevent us from understanding others' perspectives.

## What Does All of This Have to Do with Reading!?

In the same way we sometimes forget to look carefully at who we are when we enter a different community or culture, we can also overlook assumptions deeply embedded in what we read.

As you read, try asking these questions and jot down some notes:

- Who wrote this? What is their identity and perspective?

- Who is at the center of this reading?

- Whose voice is absent from this reading?

- Are the heroes or victors in this story of a particular identity? Are the victims or villains of a particular identity? Do these characters uphold or break from stereotypes you are familiar with?

- Who benefits or is harmed from the story being written this way?

- If the story is being written with a particular position in mind, and this reading is being portrayed as true for everyone, what does this mean for those whose perspective is not being included?

If you're using the free downloadable note-taking template from gutsycollege.com, I recommend adding some of these questions to the sidebar so you remember to think about them as you read.

To take this way of reading up a notch, you might also ask these sorts of questions about your class as a whole. These might include:

- Does the set of readings for each of your classes suggest that certain types of people are the primary authorities in your field?

- Is there a diversity of voices across all the readings in your class?

- Do the research articles you are reading reach their conclusions after only including certain types of participants in their pool of subjects?

You don't need to be a community organizer in Southeast Chicago or venture into a different culture than you grew up in to recognize how powerfully we're shaped by our context (though don't miss the opportunity to go if you can!). Asking reflexive questions will not only help you see new things in your college reading (and likely impress your professor with your insightful reflections), but will also challenge you to see yourself and the world in a much bigger way.

# Resonant Reading

Have you ever been carried away? Like at a concert where you were so into the music that you sort of lost track of time? Or you went out to your garden to pull weeds or to your garage to work on your car at 9 a.m. and then suddenly realized the sun was going down? Or you were playing a video game you love or driving and listening to music or enjoying your favorite podcast or e-book? There are lots of ways to be carried away.

## *What Are Resonant Readings?*

Resonant readings are the things you read that you get sucked into. These are the times when you begin reading and then suddenly you look up and realize two hours have gone by when you only intended to read for thirty minutes before getting dinner ready.

This idea of resonant readings reminds me of Franz Kafka's reflection penned to a friend in 1904 that reads, in part,

> "I think we ought to read only the kind of books that wound us. If the book we're reading doesn't wake us up with a blow to the head, what are we reading for? ... We need books that affect us like a disaster, that grieve us

deeply, like the death of someone we loved more than ourselves, like a suicide. A book must be the axe for the frozen sea within us."[45]

This might sound a bit extreme, but you get the idea. Not everything we read will bite or sting us. And it doesn't mean that we should abandon reading things like auto manuals or our kids' homework that rarely give us this blow to the head. Buuuuut ... some things will reach out and grab us. Resonant readings are the things we read that for some reason really strike a chord. And if we pay careful attention to them, they have the power to shape us, our thinking, and the way we view the world.

## Stop!

I suspect that most of the time, when we get swept into a resonant reading, we enjoy it, are maybe a bit surprised by how much it seemed to reach into us, but then quickly move on to the next thing.

Neglecting a resonant reading is a missed opportunity. Encountering a resonant reading is a rare invitation to stop and wonder. When we read something that really connects with us, it is because it is touching something important in our heart and mind. There's something about these words that shows us something about ourselves that we didn't realize.

## Wrestling with Resonant Readings

After we've recognized that something about this reading is catching our attention in a unique way, what do we do? How do we begin to understand what resonant readings might mean for us? Try asking yourself these questions and see where they might lead:

- What might this be telling me about my "why?"
  Many of us struggle with the "What am I supposed to do with my life?!" question. We wrestle to find a sense of meaning and clarity. In fact, Viktor Frankl, a Jewish psychologist who survived the Holocaust, suggests that a sense of personal meaning is essential for human survival.[46] What about this reading might be speaking to your sense of personal meaning and what you might be doing with your life?

- What might this be telling me about my direction?
  This might be a moment to stop and think specifically about what you're up to right now. Does this reading confirm that you are headed in the right direction with your education, work, and life? Maybe it suggests an entirely new direction or something you've not explored before. Or maybe it suggests that you don't need to make major changes but could tweak or adjust your current focus just a bit.

- Is this telling me something about my "where?"
  I've talked with friends who have reflected on how their reading has revealed that they love to work outdoors. Others have been nudged toward working with people. Others have felt deep connections with particular cultures or parts of the world. Might this reading suggest

something about your location or where you might find a sense of being settled?

- Is this suggesting some direction for additional exploration? In graduate school I found myself reading about social movements and couldn't stop. I read more and more about nonviolence, social change, and the biographies of social justice leaders because I was fascinated and enthralled. If you find something that resonates with you, use it as a compass that points you toward the next book you read, podcast you listen to, or movie you watch.

## Take It Seriously

If you're using the note-taking template found at gutsycollege.com, this would be a good place to add a couple of additional questions to spark your reflections. This is a strategy where you keep a running list of good questions to constantly ask yourself while you're reading.

Continue being curious. Keep wondering what it is about this particular book that sucked you in. Because we're always growing and our community is constantly changing, the way a reading resonates with us will probably change, too. Tomorrow's resonant tone might be different from today's. If you find a resonant reading, invite it to keep speaking to you over time. Read it again and again.

Most importantly, take the resonant reading seriously. Aside from how you decide to make this part of your life and career, don't let the echo of that reading fade away. That it struck a tone in you means something. Now it's your job to figure out how you will make that tolling part of your life. Respect the resonant reading!

# Revolutionary Reading

"If you only read the books that everyone else is reading, you can only think what everyone else is thinking."

—Haruki Murakami

In 2012, Andrew Delbanco, Professor of Humanities at Columbia University, wrote an article titled "What Is College For?"[47] Delbanco's article is short and totally worth the read. Should you not want to read the whole thing, I'll give you a quick summary.

Delbanco argues that college is about four things:

1. **College is about personal economics.**
   Although tuition, housing, and other costs have been rising faster than minimum wage or inflation, college graduates still tend to earn more over their lifetimes than those who do not attend college.[48]

2. **College is about national economics.**
   Economic competitiveness benefits when people go to college. Creativity, entrepreneurism, and technological development all rely on well-funded educational systems.[49]

3. **College is about personal satisfaction.**

   Going to college matters because it makes us happier, more joyful, wiser, more interesting people. We learn to think about the past in ways that help us craft a more creative present and future. To learn is to make our experience, relationships, communities, and future bigger.

4. **College is about democracy.**

   Democracy is built on education. If you live in a country that is set up to allow everyone in the country to vote on who their leaders will be (as opposed to one run by a military dictator who has the most guns or by a monarch whose parents passed it on to them like a really humongous inheritance), then the more educated folks are, the better they'll be at choosing who will run the country. Or, to put another way, Delbanco says, "[T]he most important thing one can acquire in college is a well-functioning bullshit meter. It's a technology that will never become obsolete."[50]

## Is This Revolutionary?

Reading may not seem like a revolutionary thing to do. But it depends on what you're reading and how you think of revolution.

American democracy was revolutionary. The idea that a government of the people, by the people, and for the people was thought, at the time, to be neither sustainable nor morally acceptable. The average "uneducated" public just didn't have the capacity to make decisions or choose leaders who could wisely lead a nation.

Despite these doubts, the US came to life. And it was born with its own unresolved violent history and moral quandaries. The land it was founded on was first the home of tribal nations. Its economy was sustained by the kidnapping and enslavement of millions of African people who were intentionally kept illiterate for fear of revolution. It was a nation whose political power was based on voting rights for only a small, white, male proportion of the population. The evolving democratic revolution to right these wrongs comes from revolutionary reading.

Consider these examples:

- **End of Slavery**
  In the face of President Lincoln's January 1863 Emancipation Proclamation, which freed more than 3.5 million enslaved African Americans in Confederate states, the Copperhead political faction resisted. Henry A. Reeves argued, "In the name of freedom of Negroes, the Emancipation Proclamation imperils the liberty of white men; to test a utopian theory of equality of races which Nature, History and Experience alike condemn as monstrous..."[51] In 1863, it mattered who you were reading.

- **Women's Suffrage**
  After eighty years of advocacy, the ratification of the Nineteenth Amendment in August 1920 granted women in the US full voting rights.[52] Nevertheless, a determined National Association Opposed to Women Suffrage organized events and distributed pamphlets arguing women lacked the capacity to offer opinions on political issues,

would cost the electoral system more money, would create competition with men, or would draw women away from the more meaningful work of taking care of children and the home.[53] In 1920, it mattered what you were reading.

- **Civil Rights Movement**
One hundred years after the Civil War, segregation and other Jim Crow laws endured in the US. Dr. Martin Luther King Jr. wrote from a jail cell in Birmingham after being arrested (again) for nonviolent protest and reflected,

> "I must confess that over the last few years I have been gravely disappointed with the white moderate. I have almost reached the regrettable conclusion that the Negro's great stumbling block in the stride toward freedom is not the White citizens' "Councilor" or the Ku Klux Klanner, but the white moderate who is more devoted to "order" than to justice, who prefers a negative peace which is the absence of tension to a positive peace which is the presence of justice."[54]

Meanwhile, staunch white Christian segregationists such as W. A. Gamble wrote, "It cannot be forgotten that the removal of segregation laws, and the consequent mingling of the races more and more, will inevitably result in miscegenation."[55] For most white Christians, fears around interracial marriage, refusal to apply "faithful" values to political structures, and blaming outside agitators for protests fomented resistance to desegregation and civil rights. In 1963, it mattered what you were reading.

Thanks to those who read and risked their lives, some of these injustices have been addressed. To make right what is wrong, we need rekindled courage and new visions of what could be. Democracy is not a yellowing parchment with a list of rights hanging on a wall. It is an ongoing, unfolding, evolving process fueled by a population who is liberated by what it reads.

Lily Alvarado beautifully captures this truth when she writes,

> "Everybody can undergo a drastic transformation and radicalization from having a lack of knowledge to being equipped with powerful voices. To have an army of words that can turn into action. To be the change we didn't even know we needed. Reading is a revolutionary act. When we read, we become."[56]

## *Looking for Revolutionary Reads?*

I learned during college and graduate school that there were lots of books I never knew existed. In fact, I suspect that many of the books we might consider "revolutionary readings" would not be found in my high school's library.

Since then, I've tried to integrate some revolutionary books into my reading routine. I'd encourage you to check out these lists and see what catches your attention:

- Haymarket Books' Revolutionary Lives Reading List[57]
- Angela Davis's Revolutionary Reading List[58]
- Literary Hub's World Voices Revolutionary Reading List[59]
- Angelina Ruiz's The Radical Database[60]
- Rage Against the Machine's Book Recommendations[61]

You may find some of the readings from these lists uncomfortable or troubling. I suspect they are not the sorts of books many grew up with. Likewise, I sometimes imagine the parents of European kids in the 1780s being a little uncomfortable when their kids brought home an assignment to write a three-page reflection paper on this bizarre, antigovernment document coming from some wild-eyed colonists from across the Atlantic titled, "The Declaration of Independence." Revolutionary reading is almost always uncomfortable.

## *It Still Matters What We Are Reading*

Knowing how books have shaped the rights and movements we take for granted today, it's hard to say that there are books that are too revolutionary for us to read, especially when every day a news feed features a new effort to ban certain books from public school libraries, rewrite school curriculum, criminalize certain personal identities, or restrict voting rights in one way or another. Democracy and the quest for human rights was founded on revolutionary readings and can only survive if we continue to read revolutionarily.

How can you incorporate these readings into your education and life?

Try these suggestions:

- One book: Reading lists can sometimes be overwhelming. Don't worry; there's no right place to begin. Look through these lists and choose one book. Maybe begin with a genre you're particularly attracted to. Biographies are good starting places because they can feel a bit more personal and accessible.

- Note-taking questions: If you're using the note-taking template from gutsycollege.com, add these questions to the list on your template page and use them to reflect on what you're reading:

  ○ What of this reading has a revolutionary edge to it?

  ○ What of this reading challenges me to think of something in an entirely new way?

- Reading groups: Get a group of friends together who you can read it with. Having others' perspectives is a great way to push your thinking deeper.

- Campus groups: Connect with an existing group on campus who might be interested in this sort of reading. A multicultural or international student group might be excited about sponsoring a reading group based on a reading you're interested in.

- Connect with a professor: Reach out to a professor to see if they would join you. You might think that professors are too busy to add another thing to their list. But … if it is something they really care about and it's a way to support students to dig deeper into important topics, they might be excited to participate.

- Online reading group: Create an online book group. Although these can feel a bit distant because you can't sit in a room together, you may find lots of others interested in joining you in a group.

- Ask critical and reflexive questions: Remember these sections from earlier? Don't read and immediately assume everything they write is true. Because revolutionary readings tackle many of the world's most urgent questions, asking critical and reflexive questions is essential. Don't get drawn into an echo chamber where everyone you're with just parrots back to you what you're reading. Test your thinking with classmates, professors, and others. Keep digging. Keep thinking.

- Move from reading to action: Don't feel obligated to do something earthshaking or world-saving. Start small. The power of action is found less in what you might accomplish in the moment as it is in the seeds you plant and the courage you give others. Small courageous actions multiply.

What is college for? For most of us, it's certainly about creating more economic stability and becoming more creative and curious people. It certainly makes an important contribution to national competitiveness. And beneath it all is a revolutionary democratic foundation built on reading radical books. Read on!

# Conclusion

There's no avoiding it. Reading in college is hard work. As we reach the end of this book, I'm afraid that I've probably not made college reading sound any easier. But then our goal here was never about making reading easier. It is about helping you become a more engaged and efficient reader so you can make the most from the hard work you are doing. It is about paring away some bad habits and helping you focus on not only what will help you get good grades, but also those things that will really make a difference in your classes and the rest of your life.

Most students, even star students, are not taught how to read in college. Because of this, we often end up struggling and feeling like we're failing. This isn't because we can't do the work or because we don't read well, but because reading in college is different. No one ever took the time to explain this to us. That's what this book has been about.

Our journey started with the very foundation of reading. Our first section took a deep look into the models, ideas, and brain research for how reading and learning work. From here, we pulled back the curtain on reading in college. We explored how syllabi work, what goes through professors' minds when they assign reading, and how different sorts of things need to be read in different ways.

Then we got to the meat of the matter by looking at how to set up our mind, people, schedule, space, and technology to succeed in reading. We also reviewed reading and note-taking techniques you can use to read successfully. Some of these will work great for you, and others won't. That's cool. Try some new strategies and use what works.

And finally, we touched on a few reading realities you might not have thought about before. If you remember these as you read, you will not only become a better reader and impress your professor with insightful questions, but they might also change the way you think about yourself and your world.

## What Now!?

Now that you've reached the end, you might be wondering, "Where do I go now!?" I suggest you do a bit of a personal inventory. Where are you in this process? A good place to begin might be Chapter 3 on setting up. How's your state of mind? Do you have your space and schedule set up? What do you need to revisit and figure out? This may mean re-examining your reading location or your understandings with your family or friends about the time you need to study.

Maybe you think you've got your world set up pretty well but you need to revisit some of your reading strategies or note-taking techniques. Are you just plunging into everything you read without asking yourself what you need to get out of this reading? Maybe you read every word rather than skimming things first and getting a feel for where this reading is heading. Maybe you're not taking notes and then wondering why you can't remember anything. Do an audit on your strategies and make some adjustments.

Another great place to begin would be to hop over to gutsy-college.com and check out the free workbook that accompanies this book. In it you'll find templates, checklists, and reading questions that grow from these chapters. Again, you can use what is helpful and forget what isn't. Either way, you'll find these a helpful starting point as you upgrade your college reading strategies.

The most important message I hope you take away from this book is that you can do it! Contrary to many stereotypes, reading well and succeeding in college does not start with being a super brainiac. It starts with a clear understanding of how reading in college really works, organizing your world, and then implementing some strategies and techniques for reading well. College success is more about discipline than IQ. If you get stuck wondering if you have what it takes to succeed in college, stop wondering. You do!

# Endnotes

1. B. S. Bloom et al., *Taxonomy of Educational Objectives: The Classification of Educational Goals*, vol. Handbook 1: Cognitive Domain (New York: David McKay Company, 1956).

2. Patricia Armstrong, "Bloom's Taxonomy," *Vanderbilt University Center for Teaching* (blog), 2010, https://cft.vanderbilt.edu/guides-sub-pages/blooms-taxonomy.

3. Ken Bain, *What the Best College Students Do* (Cambridge: Belknap Press, 2012).

4. Ken Bain, *What the Best College Teachers Do* (Cambridge: Harvard University Press, 2004).

5. Bain.

6. Malcolm Knowles, "What Is Andragogy?," in *The Modern Practice of Adult Education: From Pedagogy to Andragogy* (Cambridge: Cambridge Book Co., 1988), 400, https://pdfs.semanticscholar.org/8948/296248bbf58415cbd21b36a3e4b37b9c08b1.pdf.

7. Allison Friederichs, "How the Adult Brain Learns: The Importance of Creating Enriched Environments When Teaching," *Unbound: Reinventing Higher Education* (blog), accessed January 3, 2023, https://unbound.upcea.edu/innovation/contemporary-learners/how-the-adult-brain-learns-the-importance-of-creating-enriched-environments-when-teaching.

8. Rashmi Singanamalli, "Understanding the Iceberg Model of Culture to Drive Organizational Success," *Empuls* (blog), April 7, 2022, https://blog.empuls.io/iceberg-model-of-culture.

9. Aditya Shukla, "Brain-Based Learning: Theory, Strategies, and Concepts," *Cognition Today: Inside Your Mind* (blog), February 8, 2023, https://cognitiontoday.com/brain-based-learning-theory-strategies-and-concepts.

   Renate Nummela Caine and Geoffrey Caine, "Understanding a Brain-Based Approach to Learning and Teaching," *Educational Leadership* 48, no. 2 (1990): 66–70.

10. Dale M. Kushner, "Feeling and Thinking: How Both Logic and Emotion Shape Who We Are," *Psychology Today* (blog), April 29, 2022, https://www.psychologytoday.com/us/blog/transcending-the-past/202204/feeling-and-thinking-how-both-logic-and-emotion-shape-who-we-are.

11. Cassiano Ricardo Alves Faria Diniz and Ana Paula Crestani, "The Times They Are A-Changin': A Proposal on How Brain Flexibility Goes beyond the Obvious to Include the Concepts of 'Upward' and 'Downward' to Neuroplasticity," *Molecular Psychiatry* 28, no. 3 (March 1, 2023): 977–92, https://doi.org/10.1038/s41380-022-01931-x.

12. Jeffrey M. Jones, "Americans Reading Fewer Books Than in Past," *Gallup* (blog), January 10, 2022, https://news.gallup.com/poll/388541/americans-reading-fewer-books-past.aspx.

13. Philip Babcock and Mindy Marks, "The Falling Time Cost of College: Evidence from Half a Century of Time Use Data," *The Review of Economics and Statistics* 93, no. 2 (May 1, 2011): 468–78, https://doi.org/10.1162/REST_a_00093.

14. "Automatic Readability Checker," *Readability Formulas*, accessed March 3, 2023, https://readabilityformulas.com/free-readability-formula-tests.php.

15. Sandra Stotsky, "High School Reading Levels Below College Ready," *The College Puzzle* (blog), March 14, 2012, https://collegepuzzle.stanford.edu/tag/reading-for-college-readiness.

16. Jonathan Rothwell, "Assessing the Economic Gains of Eradicating Illiteracy Nationally and Regionally in the United States" (Gallop Inc., September 8, 2020), https://www.barbarabush.org/wp-content/uploads/2020/09/BBFoundation_GainsFromEradicatingIlliteracy_9_8.pdf.

17. Dave Huber, "Study: College Freshmen Read at … a Seventh Grade Level?," *The College Fix* (blog), January 7, 2015, https://www.thecollegefix.com/study-college-freshmen-read-at-a-seventh-grade-level.

18. Doug Lederman, "Graduated but Not Literate," *Inside Higher Ed* (blog), December 15, 2005, https://www.insidehighered.com/news/2005/12/16/graduated-not-literate.

19. Dimitrije Curcic, "Reading Speed Statistics," *WordsRated* (blog), November 8, 2021, https://wordsrated.com/reading-speed-statistics.

20. Wolfson Library Team, "Speed Reading," *Wolfson College Academic Skills* (blog), accessed September 21, 2022, https://libguides.cam. ac.uk/wolfsoncollege/speed-reading.

21. Susie Dumond, "How to Read Faster: A Student's Guide to Speed Reading," *Book Riot* (blog), September 4, 2018, https://bookriot. com/how-to-read-faster/.

22. Anastasia T. Williams, "Impostor Phenomenon in the Classroom," *The Harriet W. Sheridan Center for Teaching and Learning* (blog), accessed October 1, 2022, https://www.brown.edu/sheridan/ impostor-phenomenon-classroom.

23. Meg Embry, "Ask an Expert: Imposter Syndrome in College," *Best Colleges* (blog), March 29, 2022, https://www.bestcolleges.com/ careers/imposter-syndrome-in-college.

24. Williams, "Impostor Phenomenon in the Classroom."

25. Christina Vercelletto, "The 12 Best Academic Planners to Help Students Crush Their Goals in 2023, According to Experts," *CNN Underscored* (blog), August 2, 2023, https://www.cnn.com/ cnn-underscored/home/best-academic-planners.

26. "Academic Wall Calendars," *At-A-Glance*, accessed December 8, 2022, https://www.ataglance.com/c/planners-calendars/wall-calendars/ academic-wall-calendars/?srt=relevance&flt=1134-yearly&rslt=24.

27. Thad Thompson, "7 Best Student Planner Apps," *Calendy* (blog), January 21, 2022, https://calendly.com/blog/ best-planner-apps-for-students.

28. Locke Hughes, "The Difference between Physical and Mental Fatigue, Explained," *Shape* (blog), April 5, 2022, https://www.shape.com/ lifestyle/mind-and-body/how-tell-tired-or-lazy-workout-motivation.

29. Adrienne Santos-Longhurst and Crystal Raypole, "How to Treat and Prevent Mental Exhaustion," *Healthline* (blog), March 21, 2023, https://www.healthline.com/health/mental-exhaustion.

30. Housing & Residential Education, "Roommate Agreement Form" (University of South Florida), accessed July 5, 2022, https://www.usf. edu/housing/documents/roommate-agreement-form.pdf.

31. Ann O'Connell, "Roommate Agreements," *NOLO* (blog), accessed August 8, 2022, https://www.nolo.com/legal-encyclopedia/renting-house-apartment-with-roommates-29865-2.html.

32. Jill Barshay, "Evidence Increases for Reading on Paper Instead of Screens," *The Hechinger Report* (blog), August 12, 2019, https://hechingerreport.org/evidence-increases-for-reading-on-paper-instead-of-screens.

33. Emily Laurence, "Does Listening to a Book Have the Same Brain Benefits as Reading? Here's What a Neuroscientist Has To Say," *Well+Good* (blog), August 6, 2021, https://www.wellandgood.com/reading-versus-listening.

34. ENT Team, "5 Signs You Should Visit an Ear, Nose and Throat Doctor," *ENT Physicians, Inc.* (blog), July 16, 2018, https://entphysiciansinc.com/5-signs-you-should-visit-an-ear-nose-and-throat-doctor.

35. "Handwriting vs Typing: Which Is the Better Note-Taking Method?," *The Global Scholars* (blog), October 19, 2022, https://theglobalscholars.com/handwriting-vs-typing-which-is-the-better-note-taking-method.

36. Tara East, "How to Not Feel Guilty About Reading During the Day," *Taraeast.com* (blog), January 8, 2020, https://taraeast.com/2020/01/08/how-to-not-feel-guilt-about-reading-during-the-day.

37. "Top 5 Interesting Reasons to Indulge in a Book!," *FindMyRead* (blog), October 16, 2015, http://findmyread.blogspot.com/2015/10/top-5-interesting-reasons-to-indulge-in.html.

38. Jake Hostetler, "3 Reasons to Indulge in Fiction Reading (& Why It's Relevant in Business)," *LinkedIn* (blog), March 5, 2020, https://www.linkedin.com/pulse/3-reasons-indulge-fiction-reading-why-its-relevant-jake-hostetler.

39. Nicola Alter, "Coping with Reading Guilt in 7 Easy Steps," *Fantasy-Faction* (blog), October 27, 2017, http://fantasy-faction.com/2017/coping-with-reading-guilt-in-7-easy-steps.

40. Elena Touroni, "Lack of Emotional Connection in a Relationship – What Are the Signs?," *Chelsea Psychology Clinic* (blog),

January 28, 2022, https://www.thechelseapsychologyclinic.com/sex-relationships/lack-of-connection-in-a-relationship.

41. Terrell Heick, "What Is Critical Reading? A Definition for Learning," *TeachThought* (blog), March 7, 2022, https://www.teachthought.com/literacy/what-is-critical-reading-definition.

42. "48 Critical Thinking Questions for Any Content Area," *TeachThought* (blog), September 21, 2017, https://www.teachthought.com/critical-thinking/critical-thinking-questions.

43. Louise Lerner, "7 Things You May Not Know About Catalysis," *Argonne National Laboratory* (blog), December 14, 2011, https://www.anl.gov/article/7-things-you-may-not-know-about-catalysis.

44. Malcolm Knowles, Elwood F. III Holton, and Richard A. Swanson, *The Adult Learner: The Definitive Classic in Adult Education and Human Resource Development,* 6th ed. (Waltham: Butterworth-Heinemann, 2005).

45. Robert Fulford, "'We Ought to Read Only the Kind of Books That Wound Us': How Literature Teaches Us to Be Human," *National Post* (blog), September 19, 2016, https://nationalpost.com/entertainment/books/we-ought-to-read-only-the-kind-of-books-that-wound-us-how-literature-teaches-us-to-be-human.

46. Viktor E. Frankl, *Man's Search for Meaning* (New York: Beacon Press, 2006).

47. Andrew Delbanco, "What Is College For?," *Continuing Higher Education Review* 76 (2012): 11–19.

48. Adam Hardy, "The Wage Gap Between College and High School Grads Just Hit a Record High," *Money* (blog), February 14, 2022, https://money.com/wage-gap-college-high-school-grads.

49. Barak Obama, "Remarks by the President on Education" (Washington D.C., July 24, 2009), https://obamawhitehouse.archives.gov/realitycheck/the-press-office/remarks-president-department-education.

50. Delbanco, "What Is College For?"

51. Jennifer L. Weber, Copperheads: *The Rise and Fall of Lincoln's Opponents in the North* (New York: Oxford University Press, 2008).

52. Allison Lange, "National Association Opposed to Women Suffrage," *National Women's History Museum* (blog), accessed March 28, 2023, https://www.crusadeforthevote.org/naows-opposition.

53. Lange.

54. Martin Luther King Jr., *Letter From Birmingham Jail* (London, England: Penguin Classics, 2018).

55. Justin Taylor, "A Conversation with Four Historians on the Response of White Evangelicals to the Civil Rights Movement," *The Gospel Coalition* (blog), July 1, 2016, https://www.thegospelcoalition.org/blogs/evangelical-history/a-conversation-with-four-histori-ans-on-the-response-of-white-evangelicals-to-the-civil-rights-move-ment.

56. Lily Alvarado, "Reading as a Revolutionary Act," *Sigma Tau Delta: International English Honor Society* (blog), May 20, 2021, https://wordybynature.org/reading-as-a-revolutionary-act.

57. Haymarket Books, "Revolutionary Lives: A Reading List," *Haymarket Books* (blog), March 5, 2020, https://www.haymarketbooks.org/blogs/132-revolutionary-lives-a-reading-list.

58. "Angela Davis' Revolutionary Reading List," *Radical Reads* (blog), August 16, 2018, https://radicalreads.com/angela-davis-favorite-books.

59. Literary Hub, "A Revolutionary Reading List from PEN America's World Voices Festival," *Literary Hub* (blog), May 20, 2021, https://lithub.com/a-revolutionary-reading-list-from-pen-ameri-cas-world-voices-festival.

60. Angelina Ruiz, "The Radical Database," *Bookshop.Org* (blog), accessed March 25, 2023, https://bookshop.org/shop/theradicaldatabase.

61. "Rage Against The Machine's Radical Reading List," *Radical Reads* (blog), November 17, 2020, https://radicalreads.com/rage-against-the-machine-favorite-books

# About the Author

**Matt Friesen, PhD, is a student, teacher, researcher, author, speaker, and equity advocate.** Matt's meandering career has given him a behind-the-scenes view of what it takes to succeed in college. After his own college graduation, he attended seminary and spent a year in Southeast Chicago interning as a community organizer. Later he pastored two congregations where he helped people of all ages figure out the next steps in their lives.

Matt went back to school later in life and completed a PhD in Sociology from the University of Oregon (go Ducks!) and taught for five years at a small private university. In addition to walking students through social-psychology, anthropology, and social change courses, he spent hundreds of hours guiding students along their own university paths.

Matt also worked in the Career Development Center of a small public university where he helped lead advising and organize cross-cultural experiences. He's traveled with extended study groups to Nagasaki, Japan, Israel/West Bank, Agua Prieta and Matamoros, Mexico and just about every state in the US.

Today, Matt works as a Diversity, Equity, and Inclusion research analyst helping the Oregon Department of Human Services better serve all the communities we work with. Together these experiences give Matt a broad perspective on the power of college to shape personal growth, academic journeys, and career planning with an eye on the importance of community and diversity.

*Dr. Matt's Gutsy Guide to Reading in College* and the gutsycollege.com website contain more than just great advice about reading. They help students set up their routines to make the most of their classes, provide free downloadable resources, reveal the best way to tackle different types of readings, and outline the best way to take notes.

Matt loves to share with students, parents, and university faculty and staff. Reach out to learn more about gutsycollege.com, speaking invitations, and quantity orders of *Dr. Matt's Gutsy Guide to Reading in College.*

In his spare time, he kayaks with the family and dog, hikes Oregon's Cascade Range, and of course, reads a lot.

www.ingramcontent.com/pod-product-compliance
Lightning Source LLC
Chambersburg PA
CBHW020247130626
46549CB00005B/2101